THE INTROITS and GRADUALS for the CHURCH YEAR

Healey Willan

Concordia Publishing House
St. Louis, Missouri

© Introits for the Church Year. 1957 Concordia Publishing House

© Graduals for the Church Year. 1960 Concordia Publishing House

© Revised Edition. 1964 Concordia Publishing House

© Complete Edition. Copyright 1967 Concordia Publishing House

SAINT LOUIS, MISSOURI

CONCORDIA PUBLISHING HOUSE LTD.

LONDON, E. C. 1

NOTICE

All original compositions, texts, arrangements, harmonizations, and editorial annotations in this book are covered by the above copyrights. The copying, either of separate parts or the whole of this work, by any process whatsoever, is forbidden by law and subject to the penalties prescribed in the Copyright Law.

PRINTED IN THE U. S. A.

Foreword

This new publication of *The Introits and Graduals for the Church Year* includes all of the settings contained in the previously published partial collections and new settings to complete the series for the church year, except for the minor festivals.

The free barring in these settings is an attempt to bring about a natural recitation of the words. The tempo should enable the singers to sing the words with due emphasis and freedom of verbal accentuation.

In the Introits the words of the psalm verse and the Gloria should be sung easily and in the rhythm of good speech. The accents are added merely as a guide. The pause at the half-verse applies only to the vocal part; the accompaniment should be sustained with a slight rallentando to cover the vocal pause.

An accidental in parentheses in the final chord of the Introit indicates that it should be sung only at the repetition of the antiphon.

The words of the Gradual should be sung *full* as far as the ℣, which could be sung by a small choir or quartet, or by a solo voice. The Alleluia should be sung full wherever it occurs, and the ℣ in the same manner as the ℣ in the Gradual.

The Gradual and Alleluia may be sung without accompaniment, which in any case should be very light and flexible. The Tract is set to Tone IV with the sixth and first endings; an accompaniment is needed here, but it should be very quiet. If desired, the Tract may be sung in the manner of a psalm tone, i. e., the intonation (A G A) played on the organ in the tenor register, the first half of the verse sung unaccompanied by a solo voice, either tenor or bass, and the remainder of the Tract by all voices in unison.

A scheme of "seasonal" framework has been adopted for the Graduals, Alleluias, and Tracts. For example: The Graduals and ℣ of the Advent season are all built upon the same framework, and the Alleluias are identical. The same principle has been used in the settings for the Christmas, Epiphany, Lent, Eastertide, and Trinity seasons. It is felt that by this method the work of the choir will be greatly simplified without losing the interest of variety.

St. Mary Magdalene's Day, 1967   HEALEY WILLAN

The First Sunday in Advent

The Introit

A. Un-to Thee, O Lord, do I lift up my soul: O my God, I trust in Thee. Let me not be a-sham-ed: let not mine en-e-mies tri-umph o-ver me. Yea, let none that wait on Thee be a-sham-ed.

PSALM   Tone VIII

Show me Thy wáys, O Lórd: and teách me Thý páths.

Gloria Patri, Tone VIII, p. 135

The Intervenient Chants

THE GRADUAL

All they that wait on Thee shall not be a-sham-ed, O Lord.

© Complete Edition. 1967 Concordia Publishing House, St. Louis, Mo.

All Rights Reserved   Printed in U.S.A.

℣ Show me Thy ways, O Lord: teach me Thy paths.

THE ALLELUIA

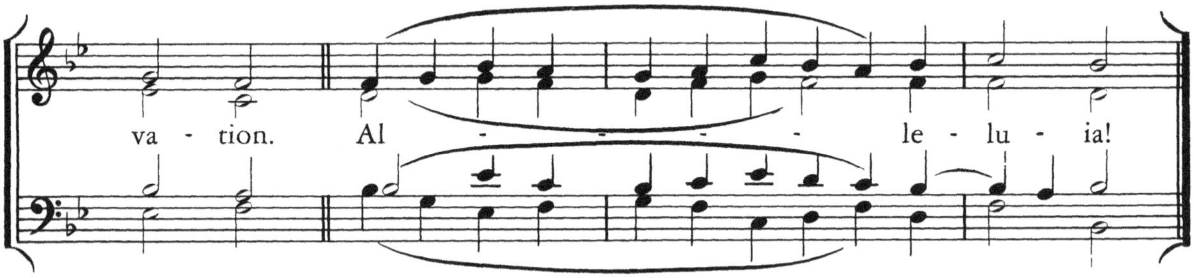

Al - le - lu - ia! Al - le - lu - ia!

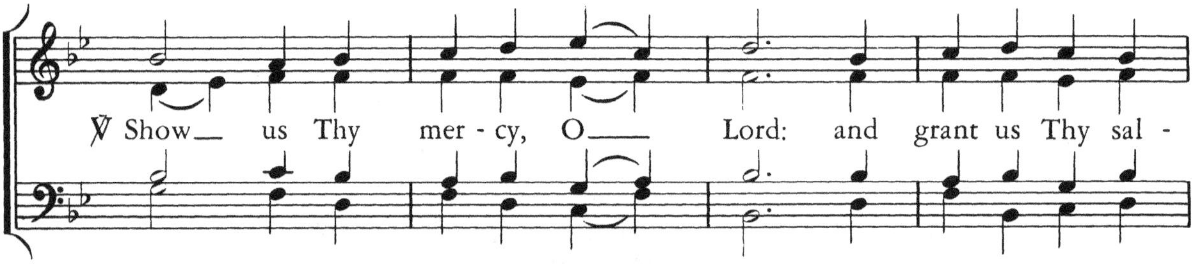

℣ Show us Thy mer - cy, O Lord: and grant us Thy sal - va - tion. Al - le - lu - ia!

The Second Sunday in Advent

The Introit

A. Daugh-ter of Zi - on, be - hold, thy Sal - va - tion

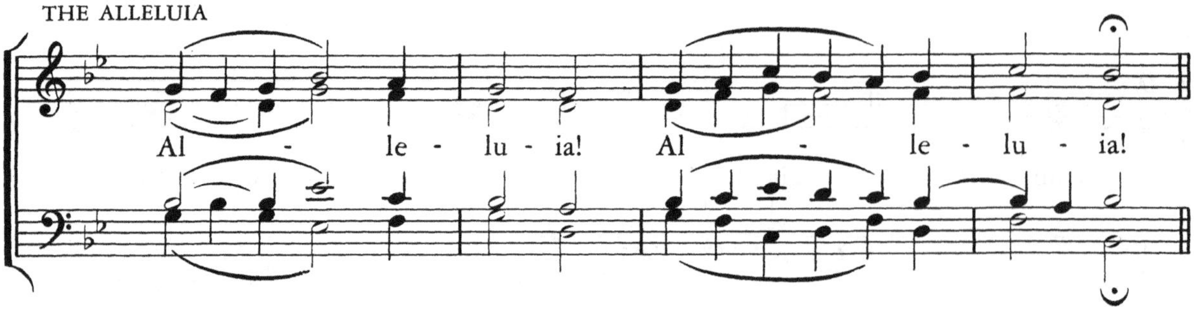

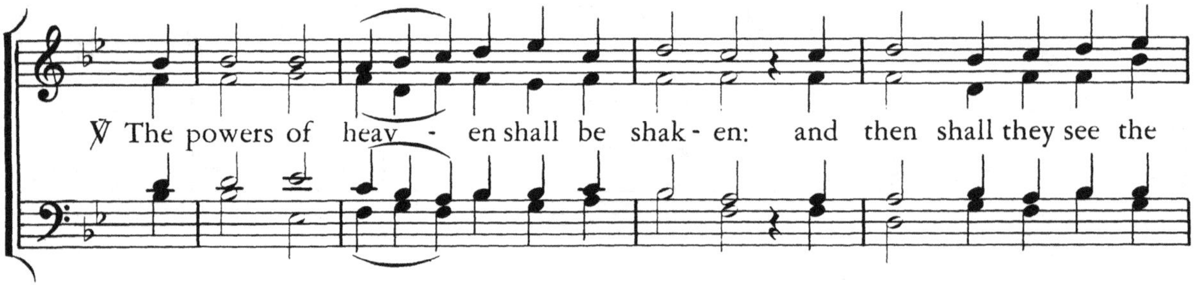

THE ALLELUIA

℣ The powers of heav-en shall be shak-en: and then shall they see the Son of Man coming in a cloud with power and great glory. Al-le-lu-ia!

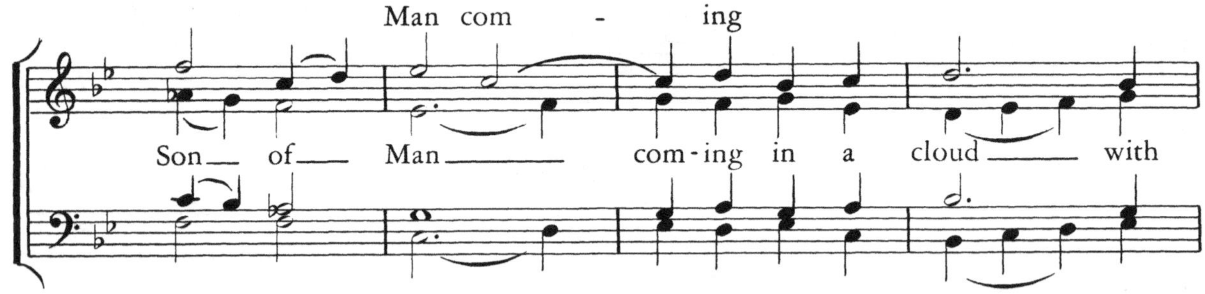

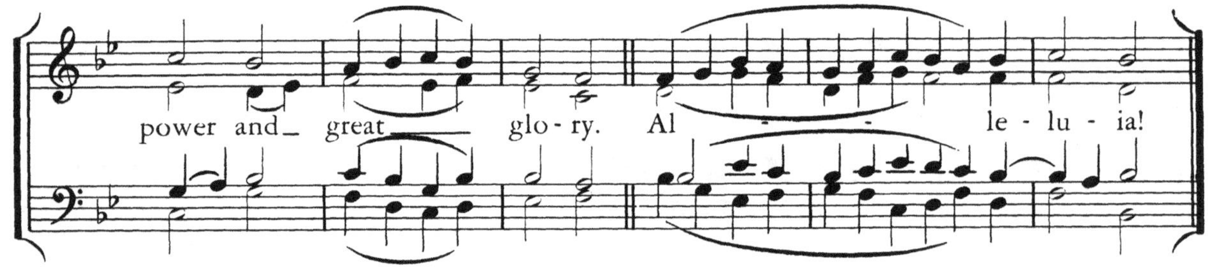

The Third Sunday in Advent

The Introit

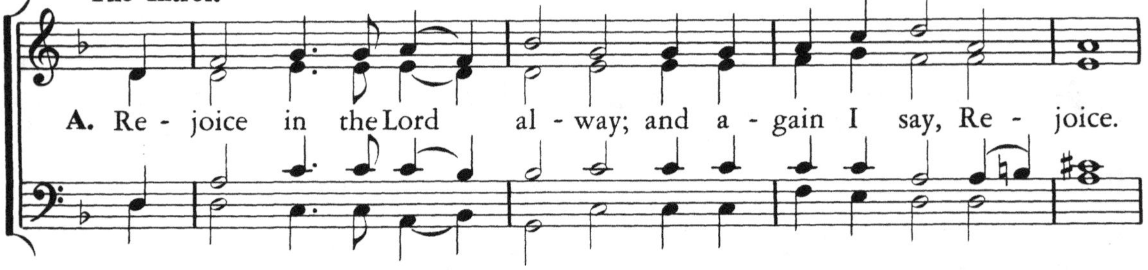

A. Re-joice in the Lord al-way; and a-gain I say, Re-joice.

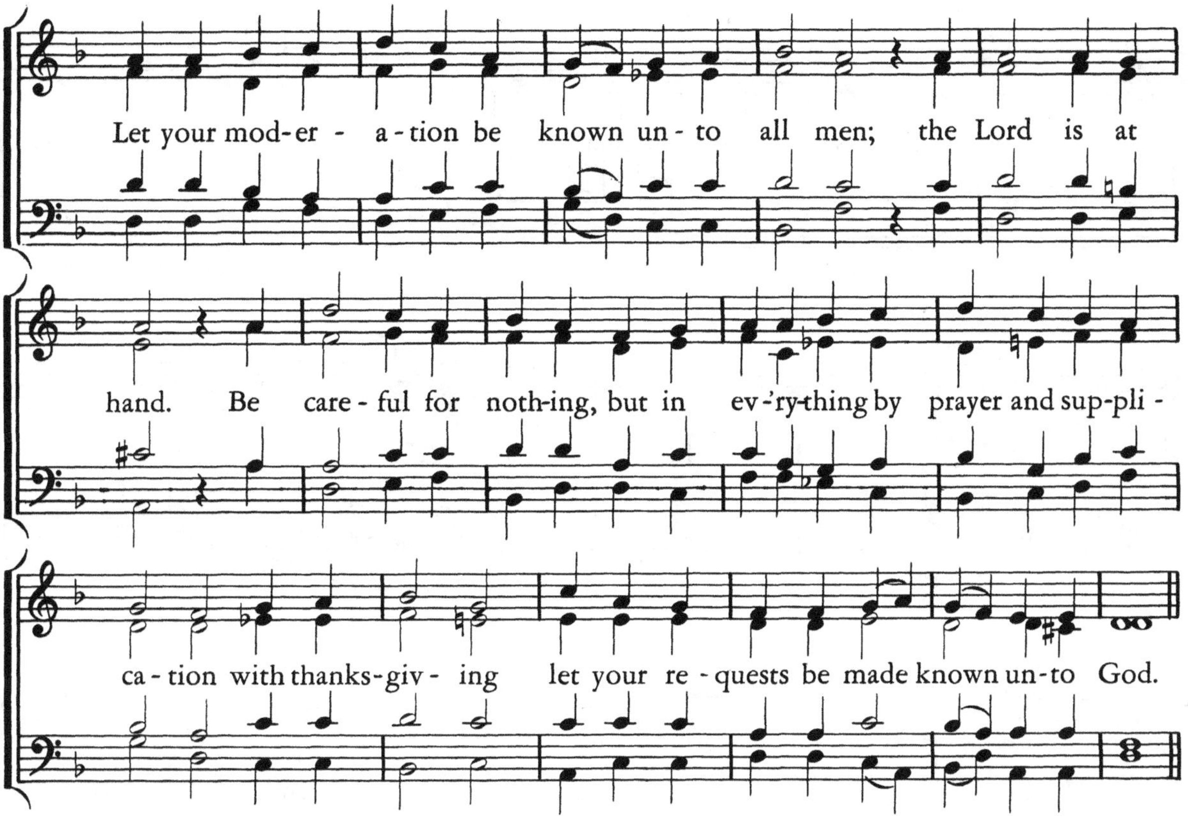

Let your mod-er-a-tion be known un-to all men; the Lord is at hand. Be care-ful for noth-ing, but in ev-'ry-thing by prayer and sup-pli-ca-tion with thanks-giv-ing let your re-quests be made known un-to God.

PSALM TONE I

Lord, Thou hast been favorable ún-to Thy lánd: Thou hast brought back the captivi-ty of Já-cob.

Gloria Patri, Tone I, p. 132

The Intervenient Chants

THE GRADUAL

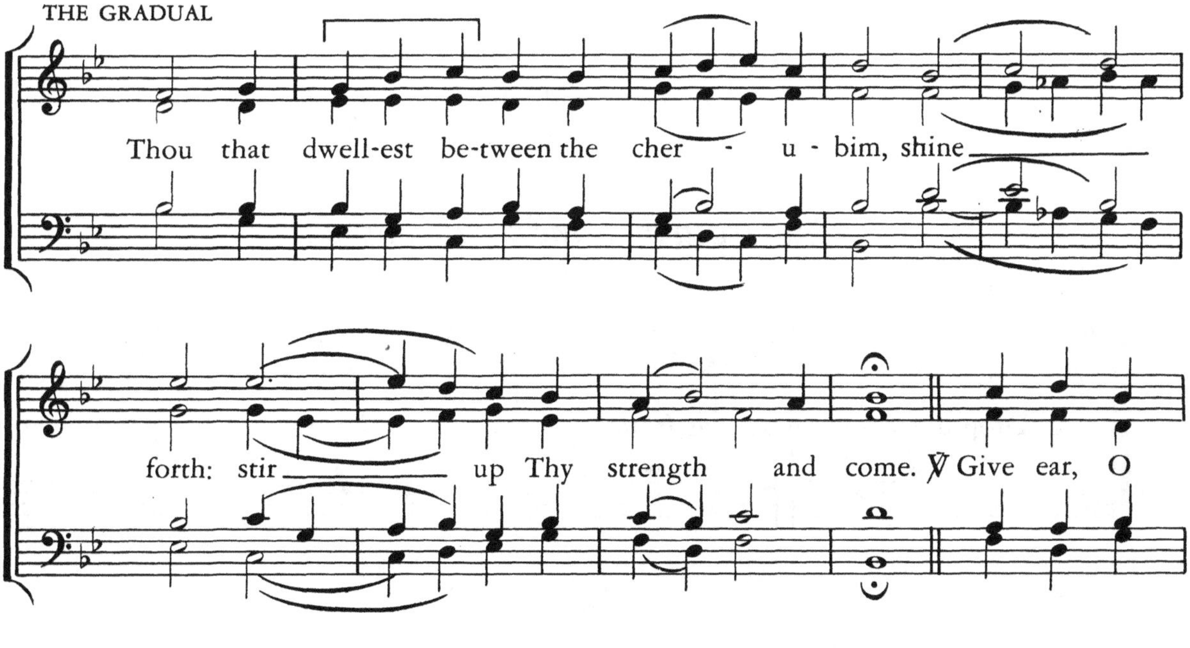

Thou that dwell-est be-tween the cher - u - bim, shine forth: stir up Thy strength and come. ℣ Give ear, O

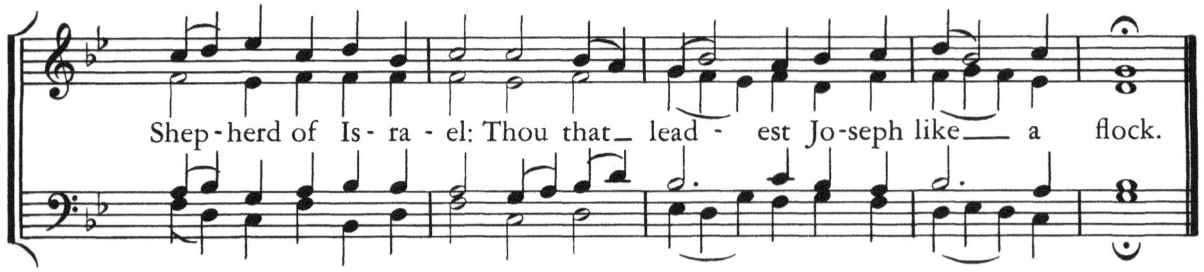

THE ALLELUIA

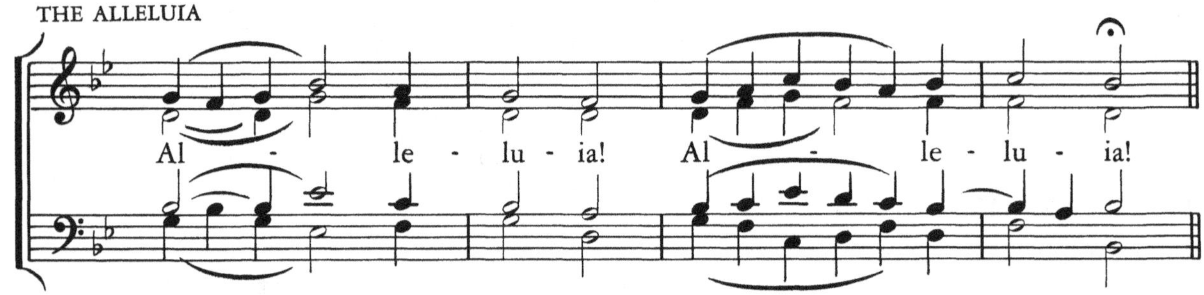

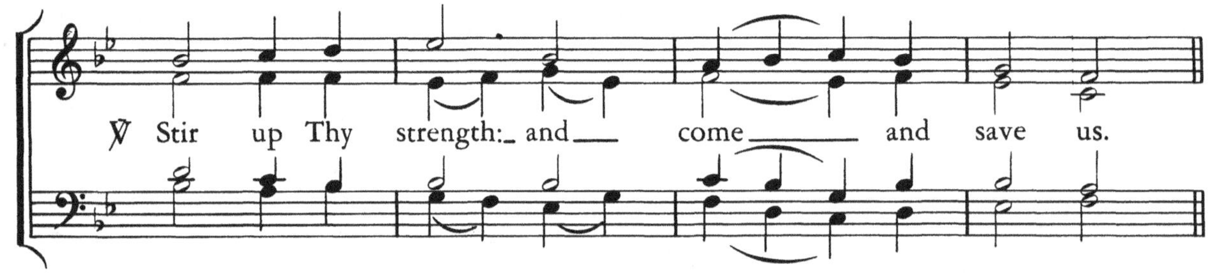

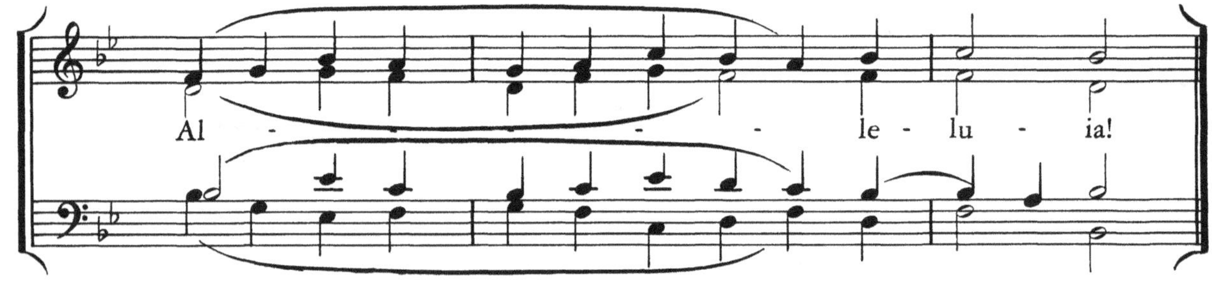

The Fourth Sunday in Advent

The Introit

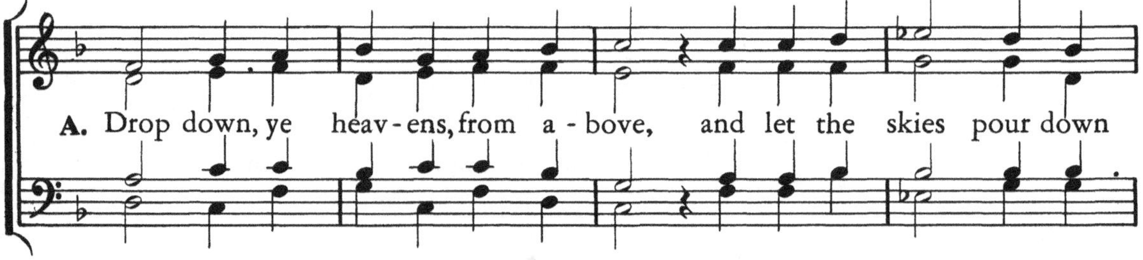

right-eous-ness. Let the earth o-pen and bring forth sal-va-tion.

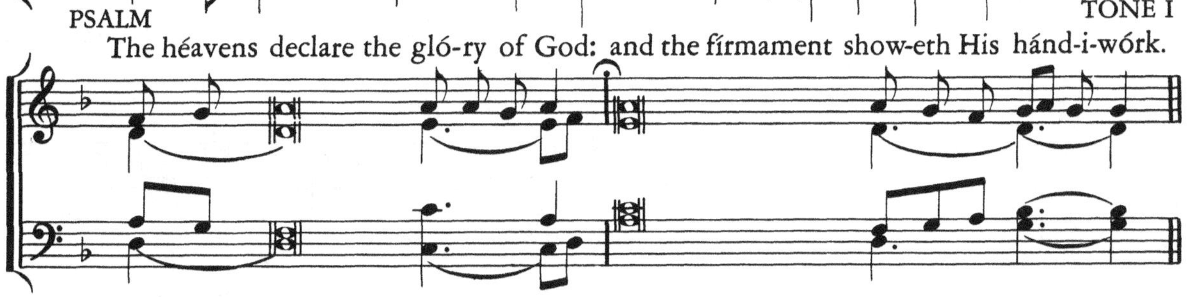

PSALM TONE I
The héavens declare the gló-ry of God: and the fírmament show-eth His hánd-i-wórk.

Gloria Patri, Tone I, p. 132

The Intervenient Chants

THE GRADUAL

The Lord is nigh un-to all them that call up-on Him: to all that call up-on Him in truth.

℣ My mouth shall speak the praise of the Lord: and let all flesh bless His ho-ly name.

THE ALLELUIA

Alleluia! Alleluia!

℣ Thou art my Help and my Deliverer: make no long tarrying, O my God. Alleluia!

Christmas Day, the Feast of the Nativity of Our Lord

The Introit

A. Unto us a Child is born, unto us a Son is given; and the government shall be upon His shoulder.

16 **The Intervenient Chants (alternate)**

The Second Christmas Day

(The Introit, or its alternate, is the same as for Christmas Day, the Feast of the Nativity of Our Lord, p. 12)

The Intervenient Chants

THE GRADUAL

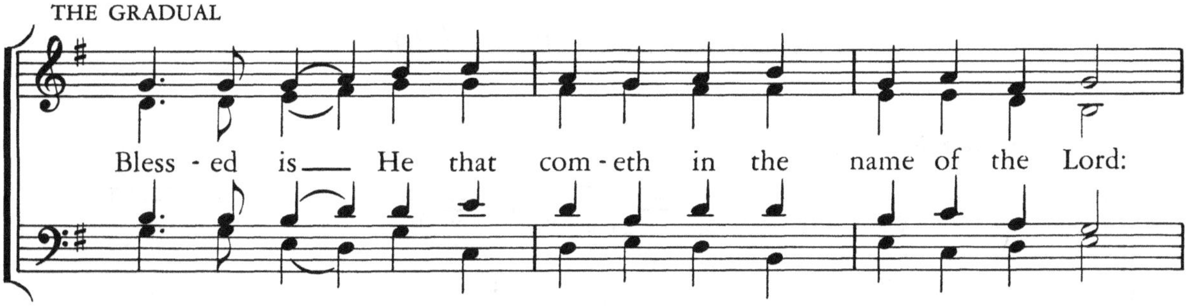

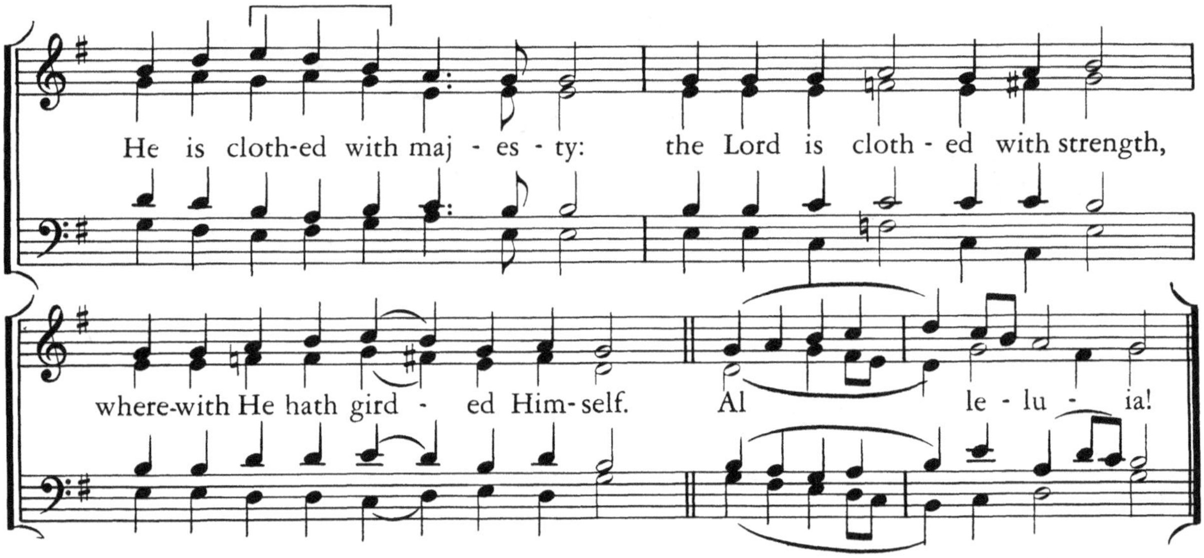
He is cloth-ed with maj - es - ty: the Lord is cloth - ed with strength,
where-with He hath gird - ed Him- self. Al le - lu - ia!

The Sunday After Christmas

The Introit

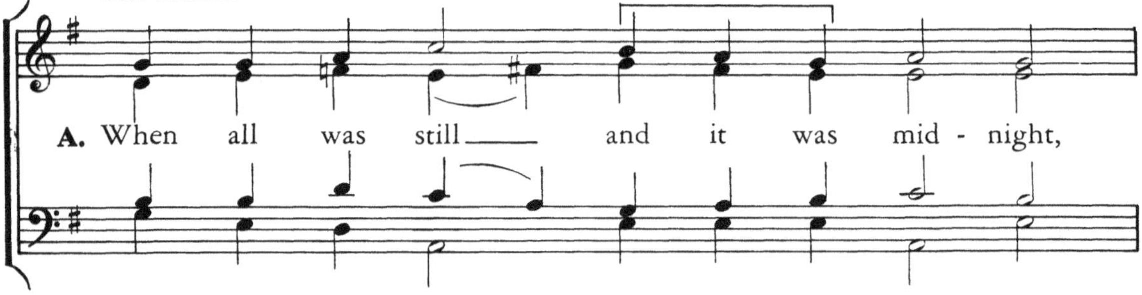
A. When all was still and it was mid - night,

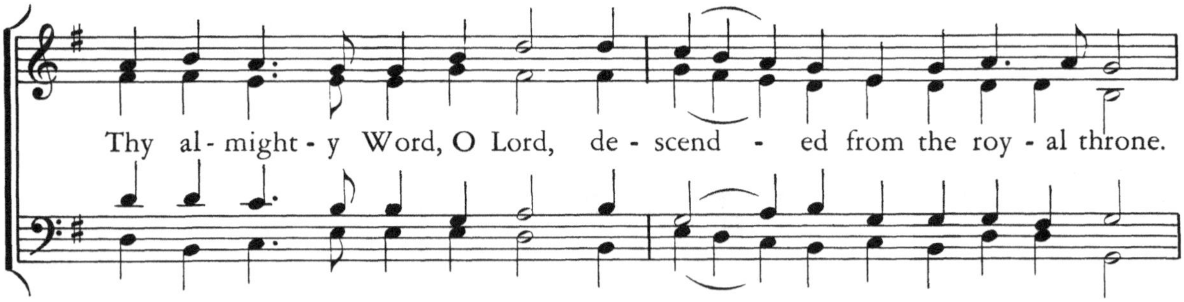
Thy al- might - y Word, O Lord, de - scend - ed from the roy - al throne.

PSALM

Tone VII

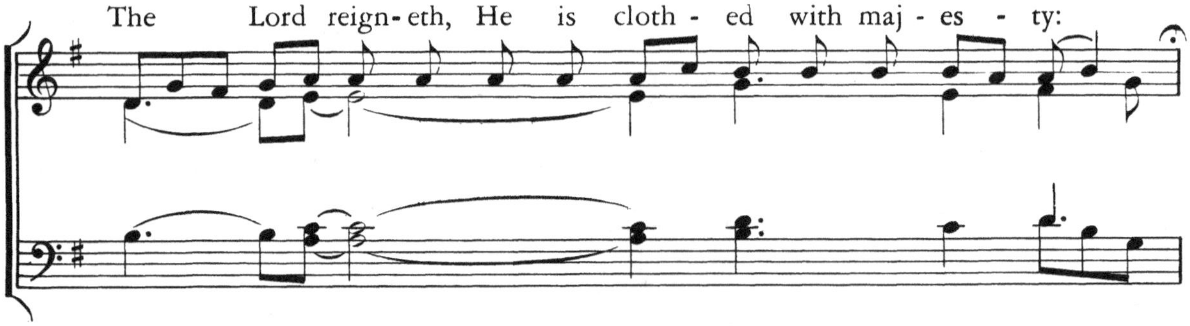
The Lord reign- eth, He is cloth - ed with maj - es - ty:

The Circumcision and the Name of Jesus

The Introit

A. O Lord, our Lord, how ex-cel-lent is Thy name in all the earth, who hast set Thy glo-ry a-bove the heav'ns! What is man that Thou art mind-ful of him, and the Son of Man that Thou vis-it-est Him?

PSALM   Tone VIII
Thou, O Lórd, art our Fáther and our Re-déem-er: Thy náme is from év-er-lást-ing.

Gloria Patri, Tone VIII, p. 135

The Intervenient Chants

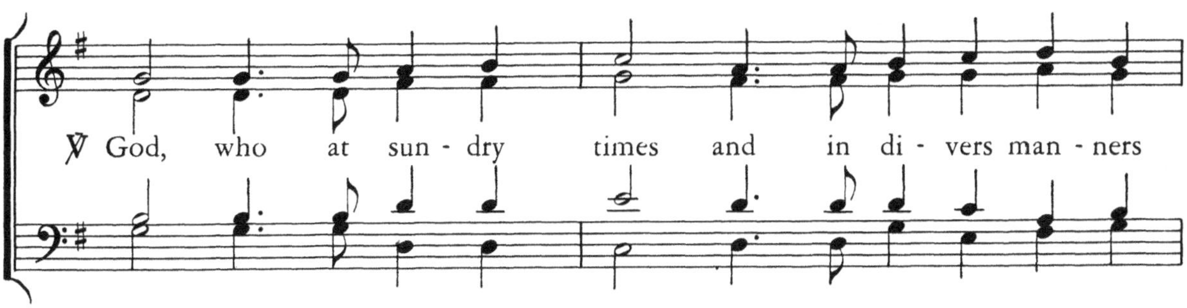

℣ God, who at sundry times and in divers manners spake in times past by the prophets: hath in these last days spoken unto us by His Son. Alleluia!

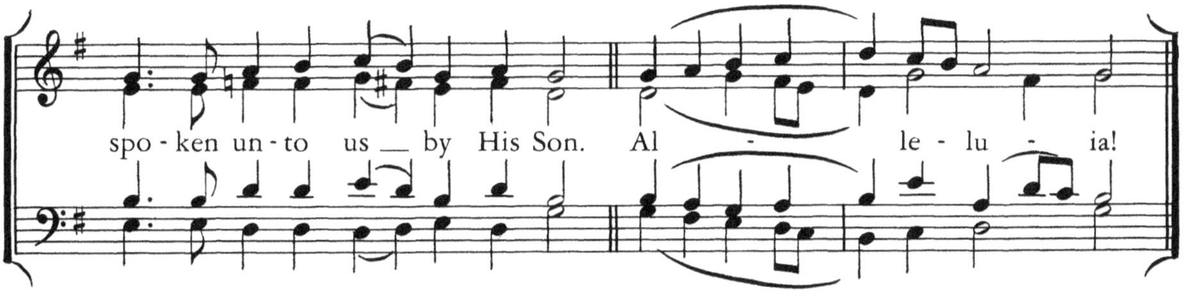

The Second Sunday After Christmas

(The Introit is the same as for the Sunday After Christmas, p. 18)

The Intervenient Chants

THE GRADUAL

Save us, O Lord, our God, and gather us from among the heathen: to give thanks unto Thy holy name and to triumph in Thy praise.

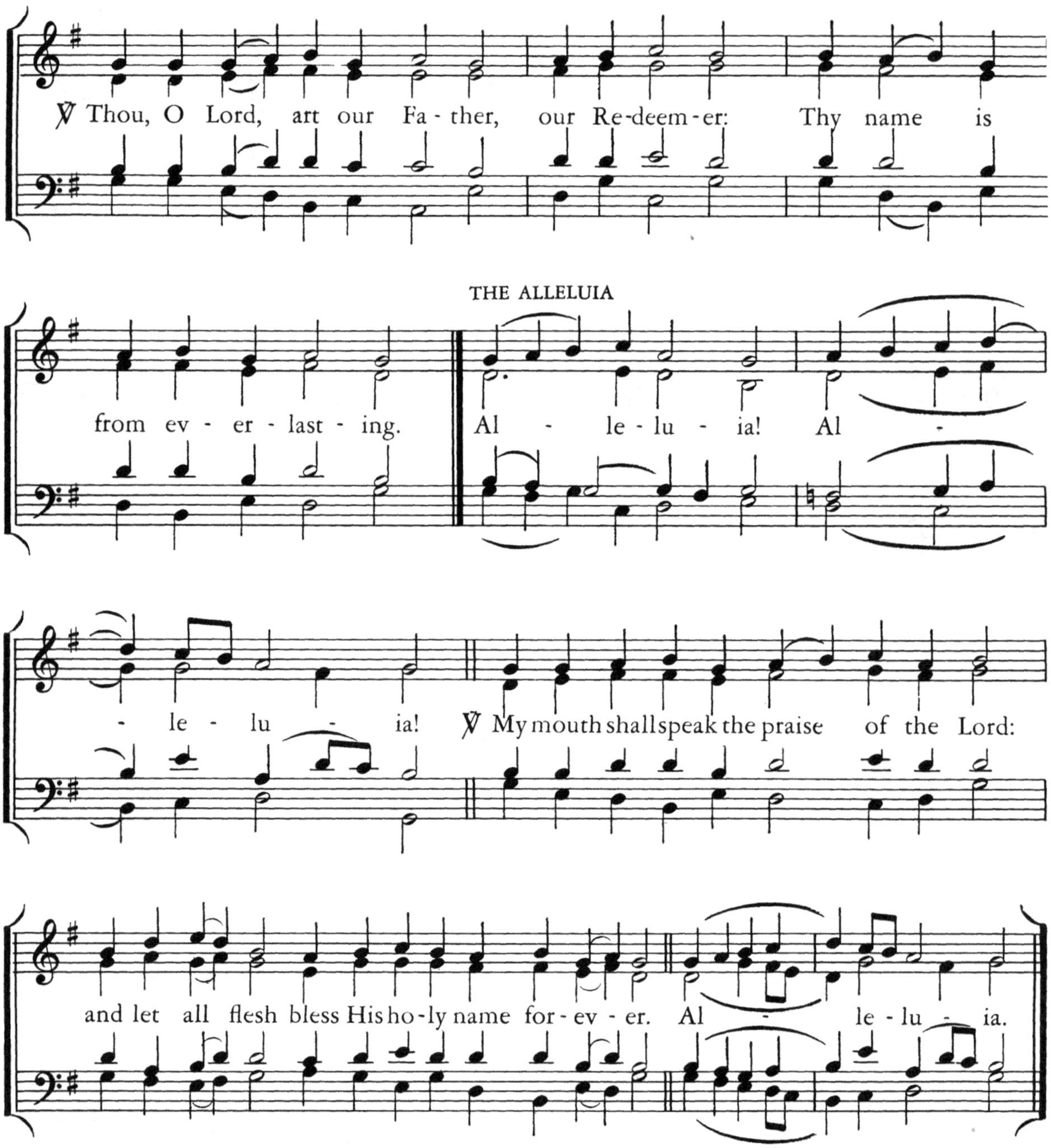

The Epiphany of Our Lord

The Introit

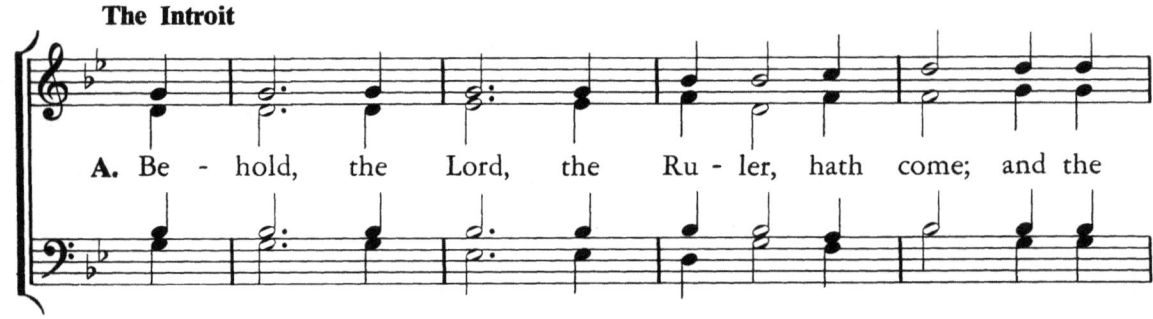

The First Sunday After the Epiphany

The Introit

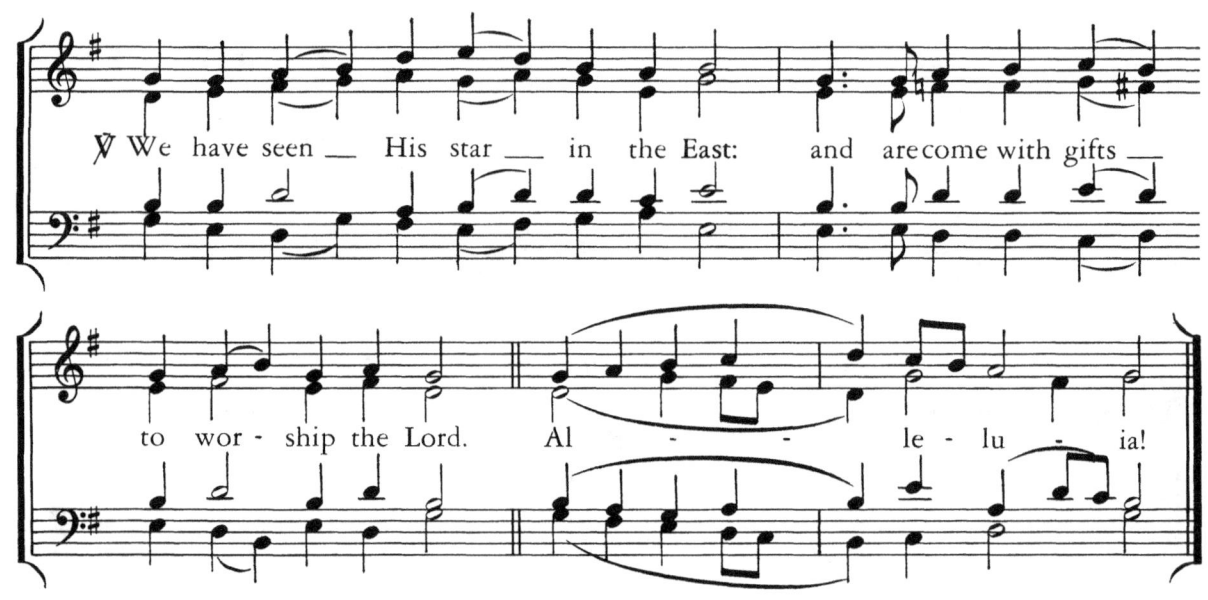

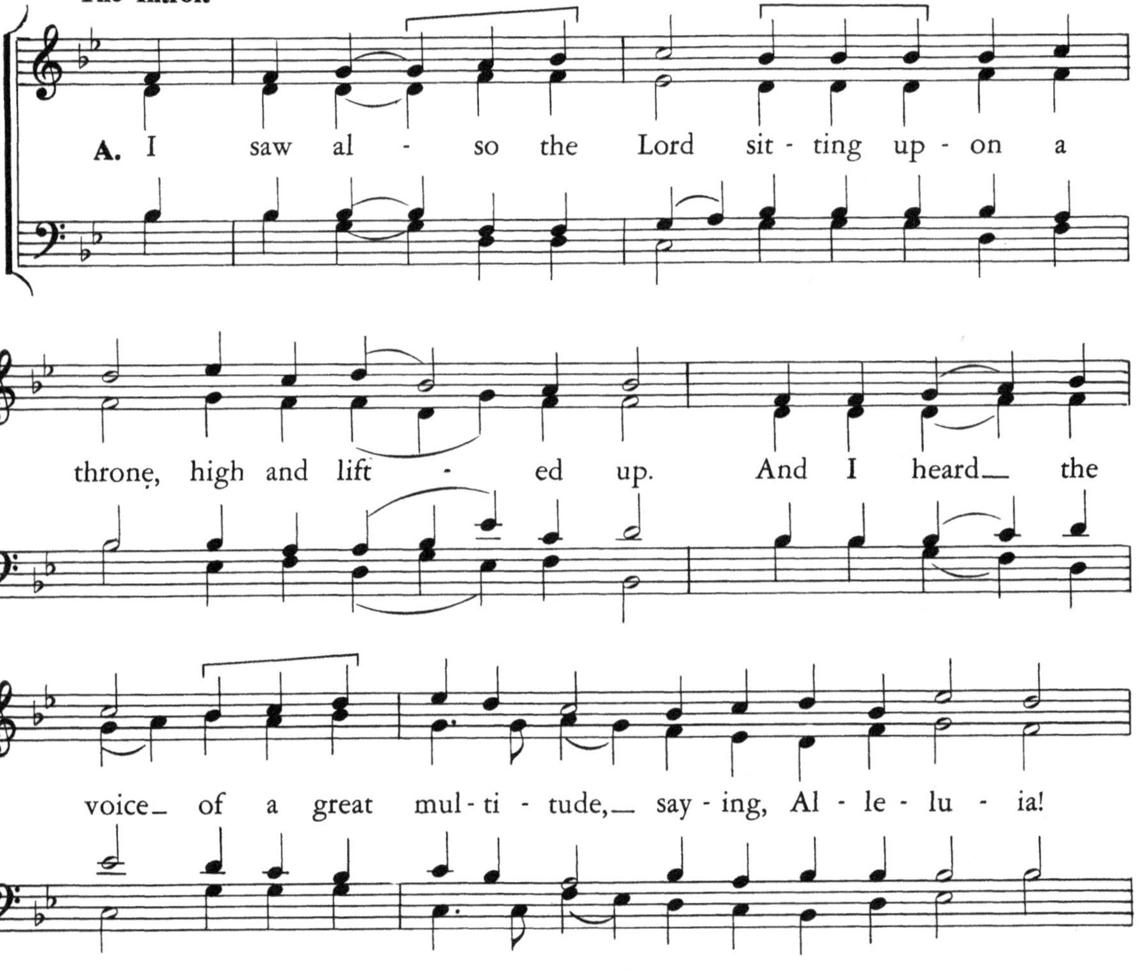

PSALM

Tone VIII

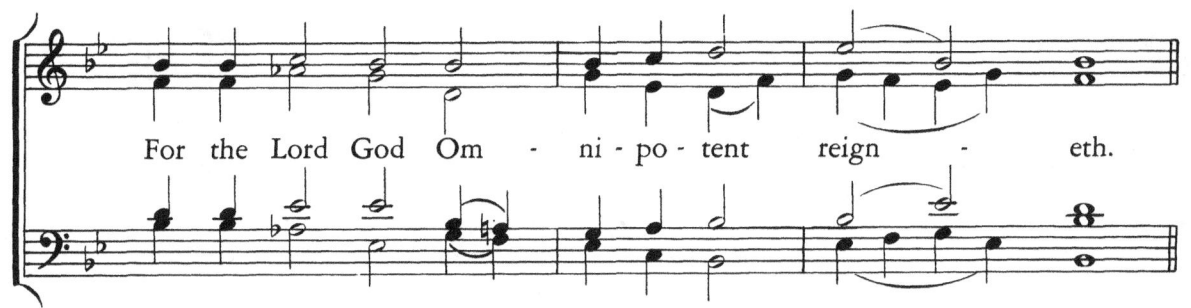

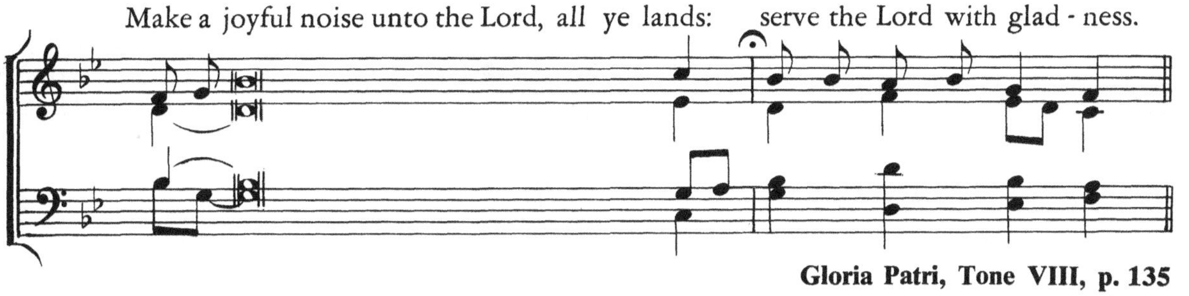

Gloria Patri, Tone VIII, p. 135

The Intervenient Chants

THE GRADUAL

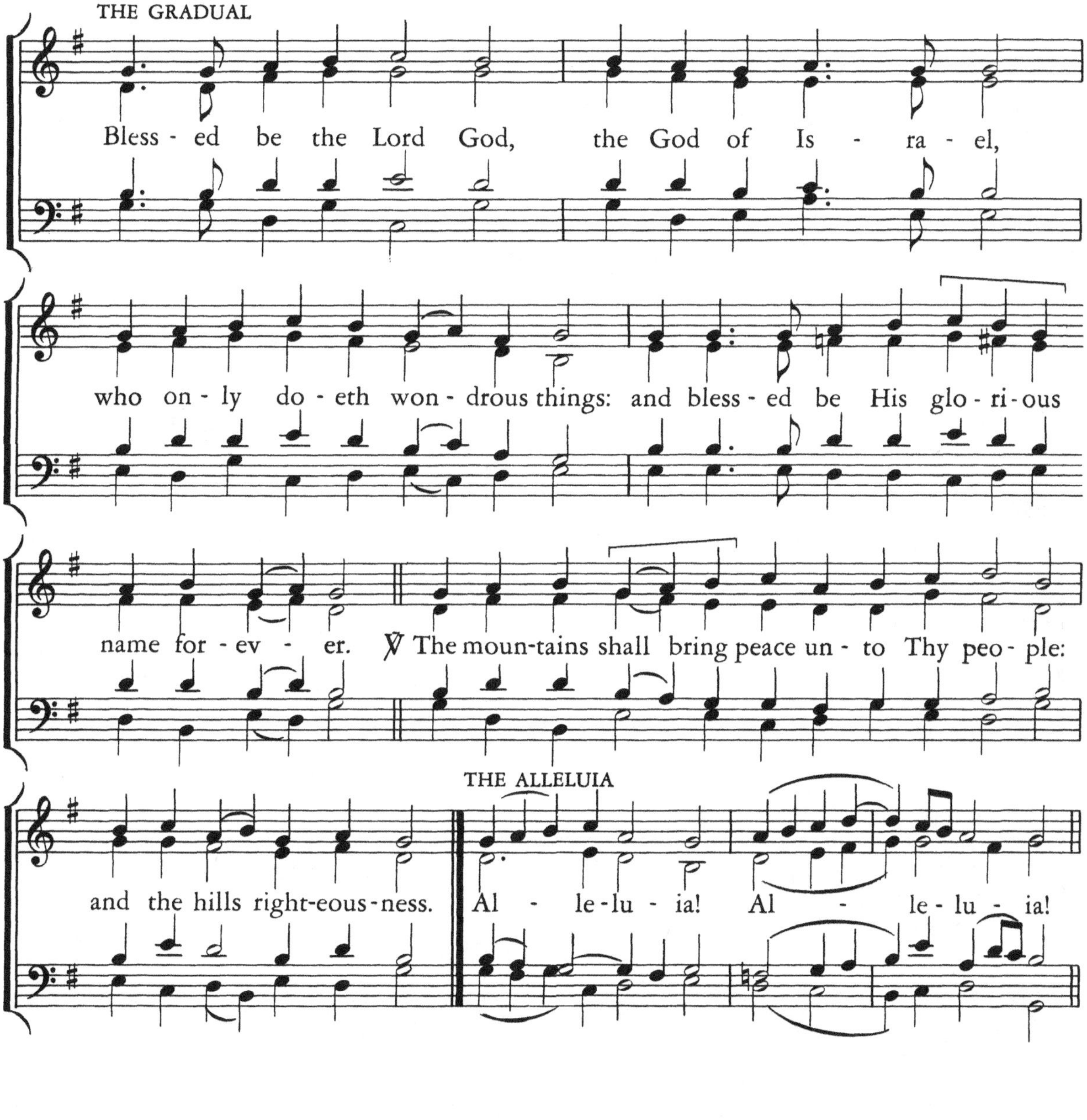

The Second Sunday After the Epiphany

The Introit

PSALM — Tone IV

Make a joyful noise unto God, all ye lands: sing forth the honor of His

name, make His praise glorious.

Gloria Patri, Tone IV, p. 133

The Third Sunday After the Epiphany

The Introit

A. Wor-ship Him, all ye His an-gels. Zi-on heard and was glad. The daugh-ters of Ju-dah re-joic-ed be-cause of Thy judg-ments, O Lord.

PSALM — Tone VII
The Lord reigneth, let the earth re-joice: let the multitude of isles be glad there-of.

Gloria Patri, Tone VII, p. 135

The Intervenient Chants

The Fourth Sunday After the Epiphany

The Introit

(The Introit is the same as for the Third Sunday After the Epiphany, p. 30)

The Intervenient Chants

(The Gradual and the Alleluia are the same as for the Third Sunday After the Epiphany, p. 31)

The Fifth Sunday After the Epiphany

The Introit

(The Introit is the same as for the Third Sunday After the Epiphany, p. 30)

The Intervenient Chants

(The Gradual and the Alleluia are the same as for the Third Sunday After the Epiphany, p. 31)

The Sixth Sunday After the Epiphany (Transfiguration)

The Introit

A. The lightnings lightened the world; the earth

trembléd and shook.

PSALM Tone III

Gloria Patri, Tone III, p. 133

The Intervenient Chants

THE GRADUAL

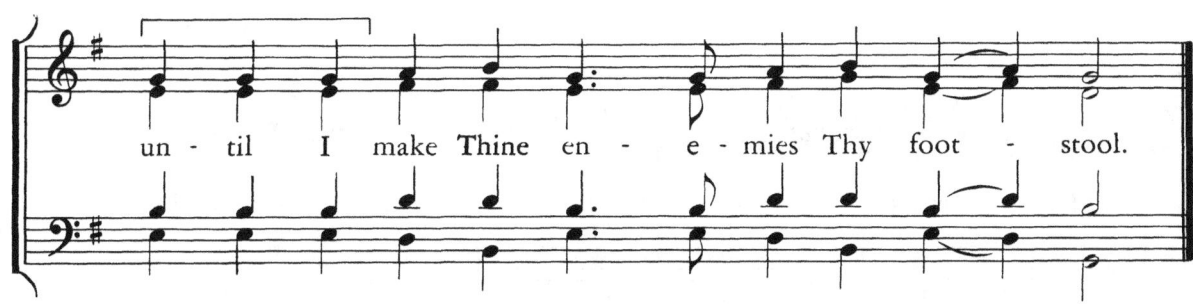

THE ALLELUIA

Alleluia! Alleluia!

℣ Sing unto the Lord, bless His name; show forth His salvation from day to day: Declare His glory among all people. Alleluia!

Septuagesima Sunday

The Introit

A. The sorrows of death compassed me; the sorrows of hell

PSALM — Tone V

I will love Thee, O Lord, my Strength: the Lord is my Rock and my Fortress.

Gloria Patri, Tone V, p. 134

The Intervenient Chants

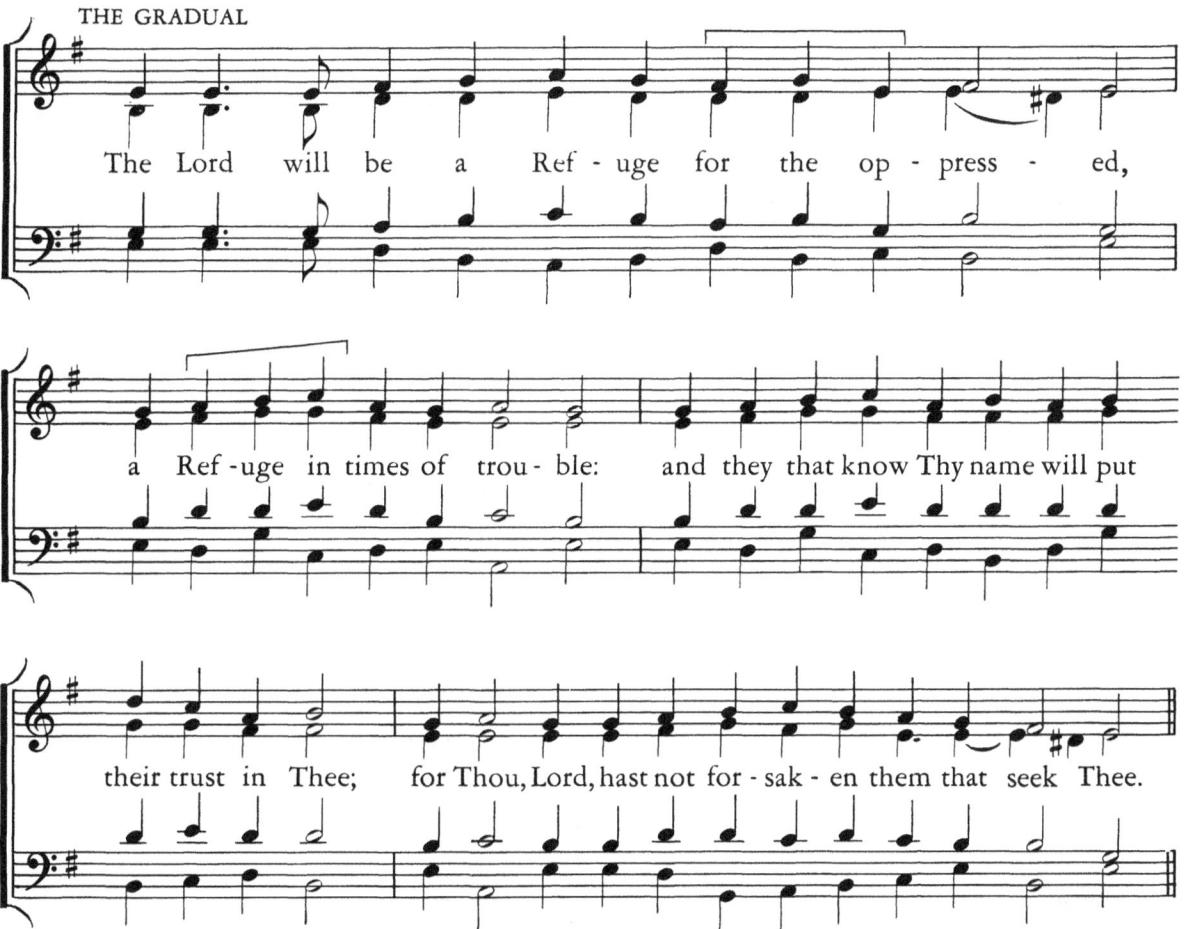

36

Sexagesimal Sunday

Quinquagesimma Sunday

The Introit

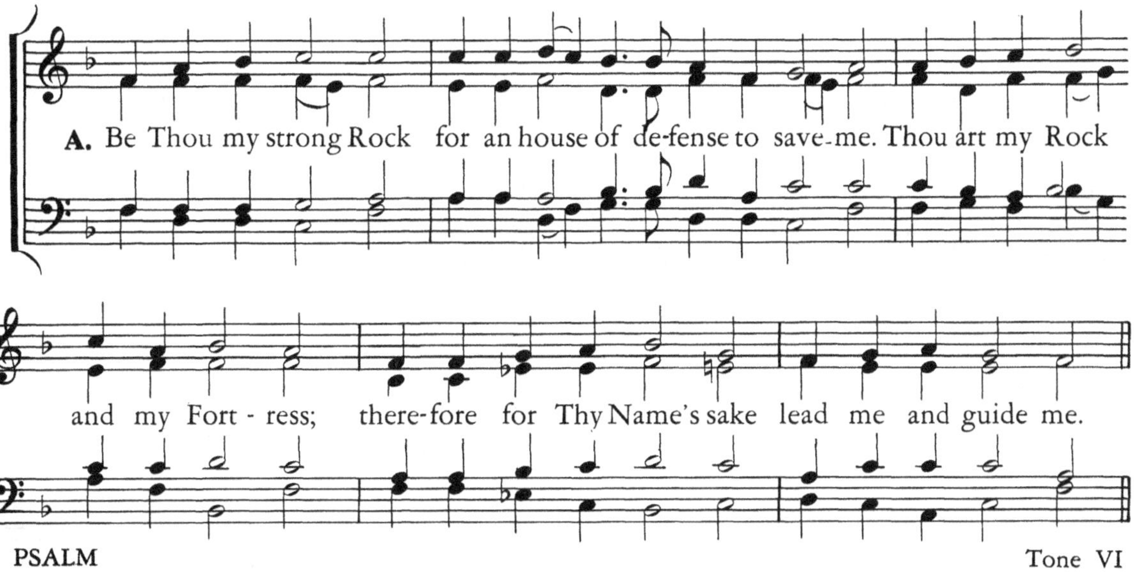

A. Be Thou my strong Rock for an house of defense to save me. Thou art my Rock and my Fortress; therefore for Thy Name's sake lead me and guide me.

PSALM Tone VI

In Thee, O Lord, do I put my trust; let me never be ashamed: deliver me in Thy righteousness. Glory be to the Father

giv-ing: Know ye that the Lord, He is God. It is He that hath made us and not we our-selves: we are His people and the sheep of His pas-ture.

Invocavit, the First Sunday in Lent

The Introit

A. He shall call up-on Me, and I will an-'swer him; I will de-liv-er him and hon-or him, With long life will I sat-is-fy him and show him My sal-va-tion.

God: in Him will I trust. He shall cover thee with His feath - ers:
and un - der His wings shalt ___ thou ______ trust.

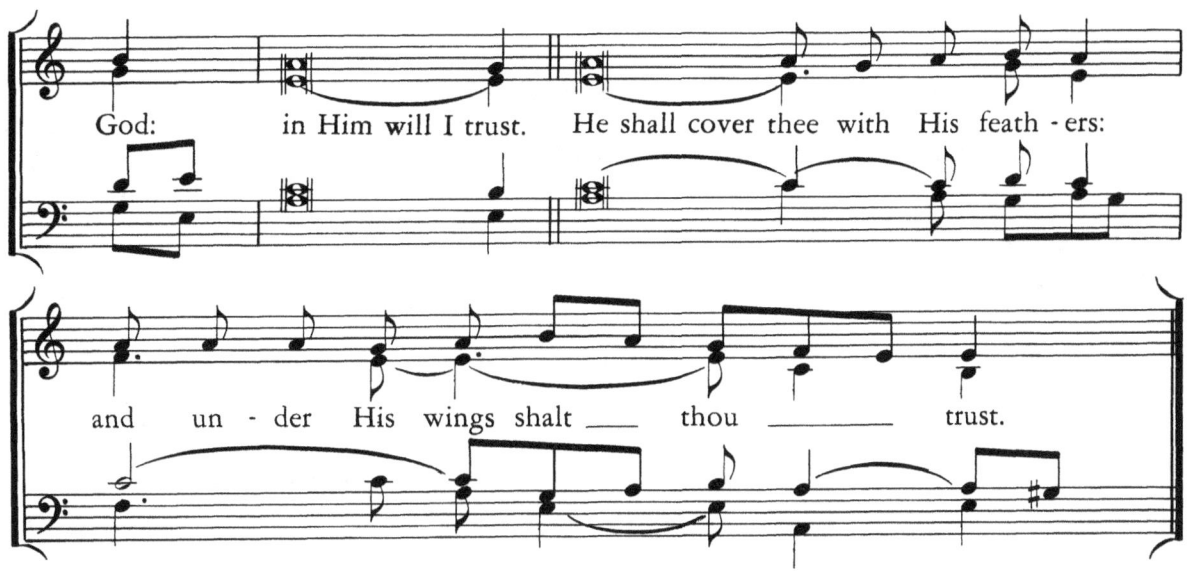

Reminiscere, the Second Sunday in Lent

The Introit

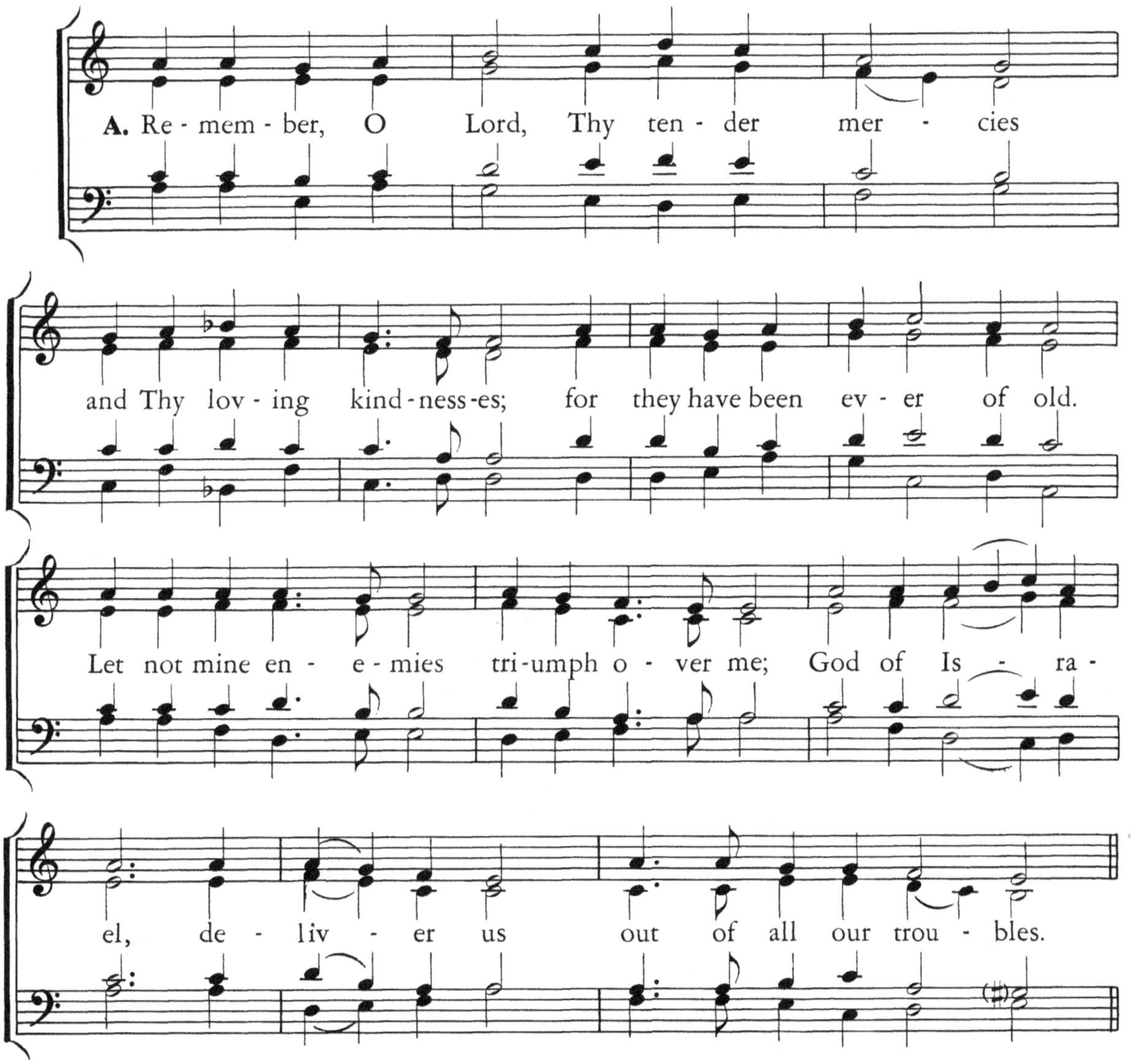
A. Re - mem - ber, O Lord, Thy ten - der mer - cies
and Thy lov - ing kind - ness - es; for they have been ev - er of old.
Let not mine en - e - mies tri - umph o - ver me; God of Is - ra -
el, de - liv - er us out of all our trou - bles.

PSALM Tone IV

Un-to Thee, O Lord, do I lift up my soul: O my God, I trust in Thee; let me not be a-sham-ed.

Gloria Patri, Tone IV, p. 133

The Intervenient Chants

THE GRADUAL

The trou-bles of my heart are en-larg-ed: oh, bring Thou me out of my dis-tress-es. ℣ Look up-on mine af-flic-tion and my pain: and for-give all my sins.

THE TRACT (Voices in unison) Tone IV

Oh, give thanks unto the Lord; for He is good: for His mercy endureth for-ev-er.

Who can utter the mighty acts of the Lord? Who can show forth His praise? Bless-ed are they that keep judg-ment: and he that doeth righteousness at all times. Remember me, O Lord, with the favor that Thou bearest un-to Thy peo-ple: Oh, vis-it me with Thy sal-va-tion.

Oculi, the Third Sunday in Lent

The Introit

A. Mine eyes are ev-er to-ward the Lord; for He shall pluck my feet out of the net. Turn Thee un-to me and have mer-cy up-on me; for I am des-o-late and af-flict-ed.

PSALM Tone VII

Un-to Thee, O Lord, do I lift up my soul: O my God, I trust

Laetare, the Fourth Sunday in Lent

Repeat the Antiphon

Judica, the Fifth Sunday in Lent
Passion Sunday

Omit the Gloria

Repeat the Antiphon

Palmarum, the Sixth Sunday in Lent

Good Friday

The Introit

A. Surely He hath borne our griefs and carried our sorrows:

Repeat the Antiphon

The Intervenient Chant

THE GRADUAL

Easter Day, the Feast of the Resurrection of Our Lord

The Introit

The Introit (alternate)

PSALM Tone V

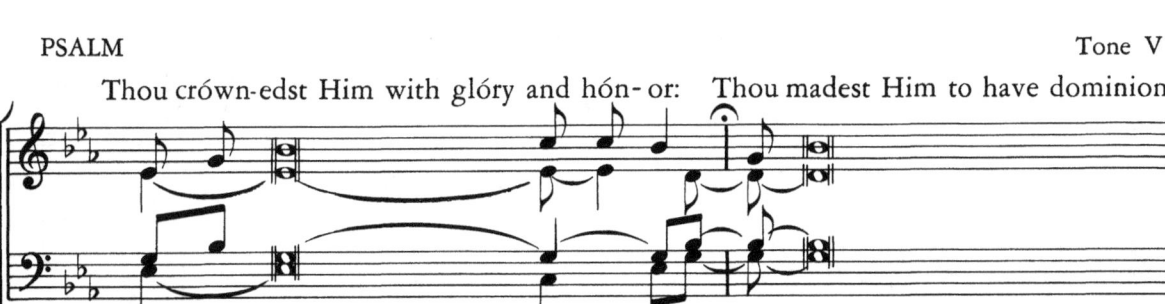

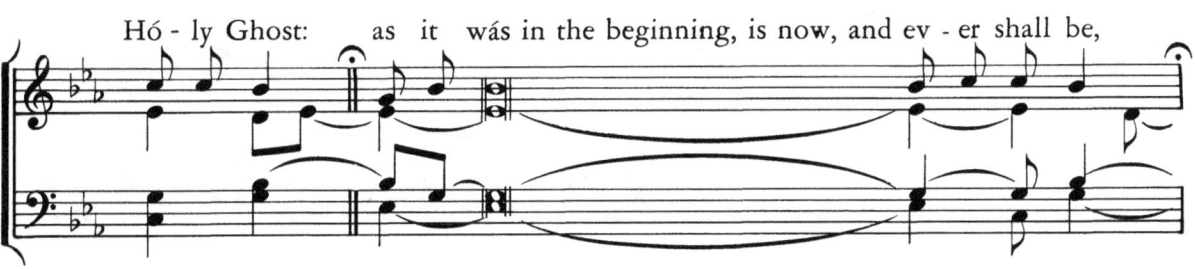

Repeat the Antiphon

The Intervenient Chants

Quasimodogeniti, the First Sunday After Easter

The Introit

64

PSALM
Sing a-loúd unto God, our Strength: make a joyful nóise unto the Gód of Já-cob.

Tone VI

The Intervenient Chant
The Greater Alleluia

Gloria Patri, Tone VI, p. 134

ALLELUIA I

℣ Christ, our Pass-o-ver, is sac-ri-fic-ed for us.

ALLELUIA II

℣ The an-gel of the Lord de-scend-ed from heav'n: and came and roll-ed

Misericordias Domini, the Second Sunday After Easter

The Introit

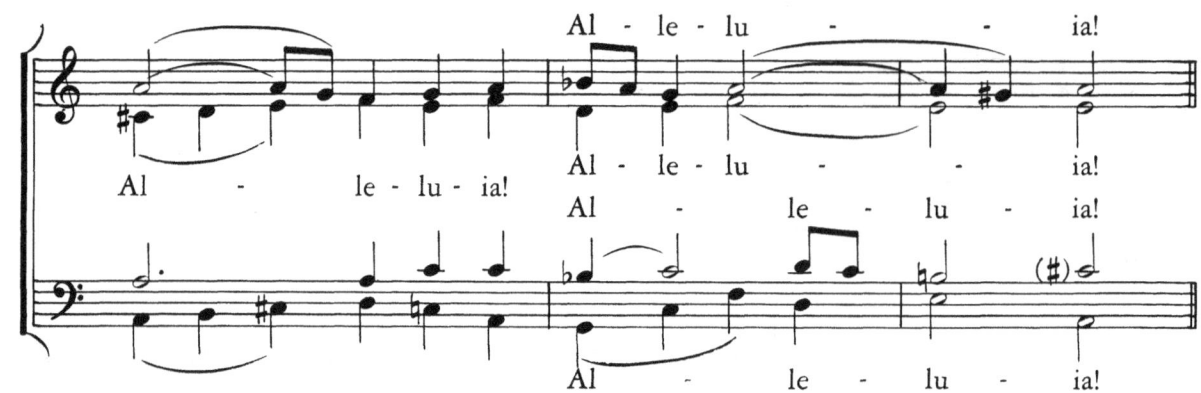

PSALM Tone IV
Rejóice in the Lórd, O ye ríghteous: for praise is cómely for the úpright.

Gloria Patri, Tone IV, p. 133

The Intervenient Chant
The Greater Alleluia

ALLELUIA I

℣ Then was the Lord Jesus known of the disciples in the breaking of bread.

ALLELUIA II

Jubilate, the Third Sunday After Easter

The Introit

PSALM   Tone VIII

Gloria Patri, Tone VIII, p. 135

The Intervenient Chant
The Greater Alleluia

ALLELUIA I

ALLELUIA II

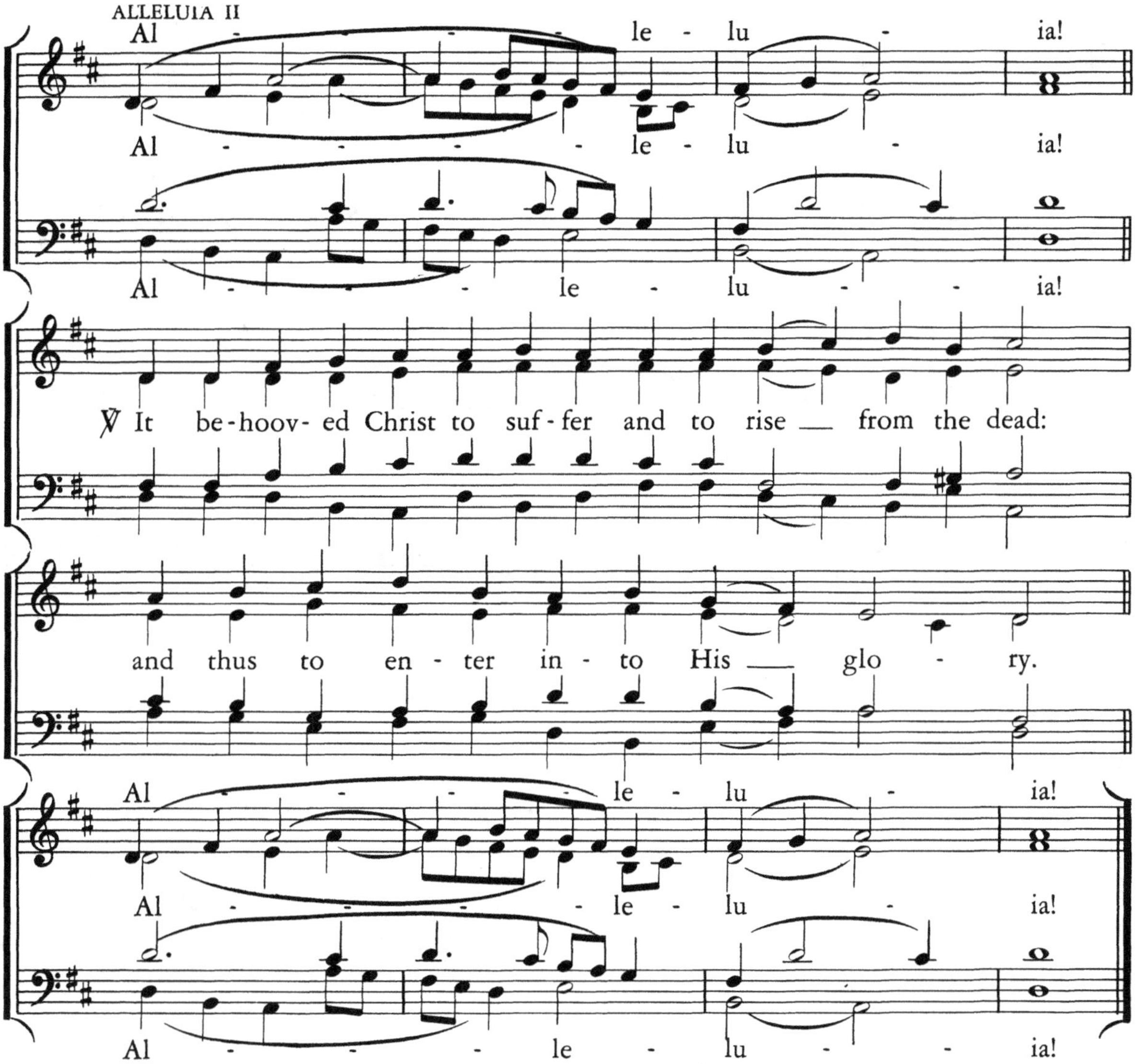

Cantate, the Fourth Sunday After Easter

The Introit

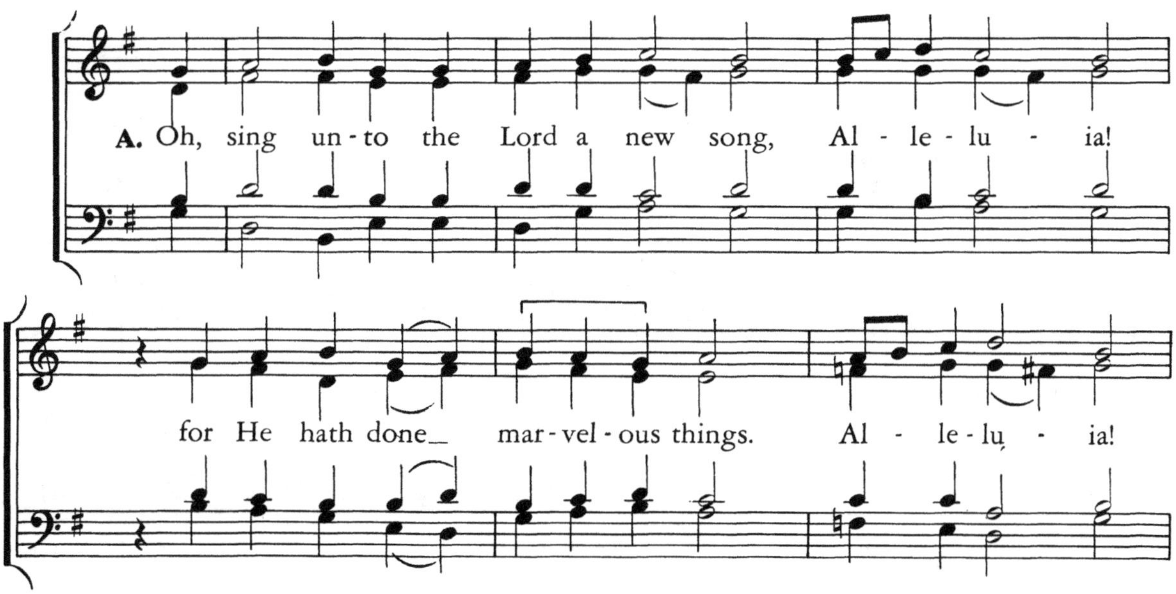

Rogate, the Fifth Sunday After Easter

The Introit

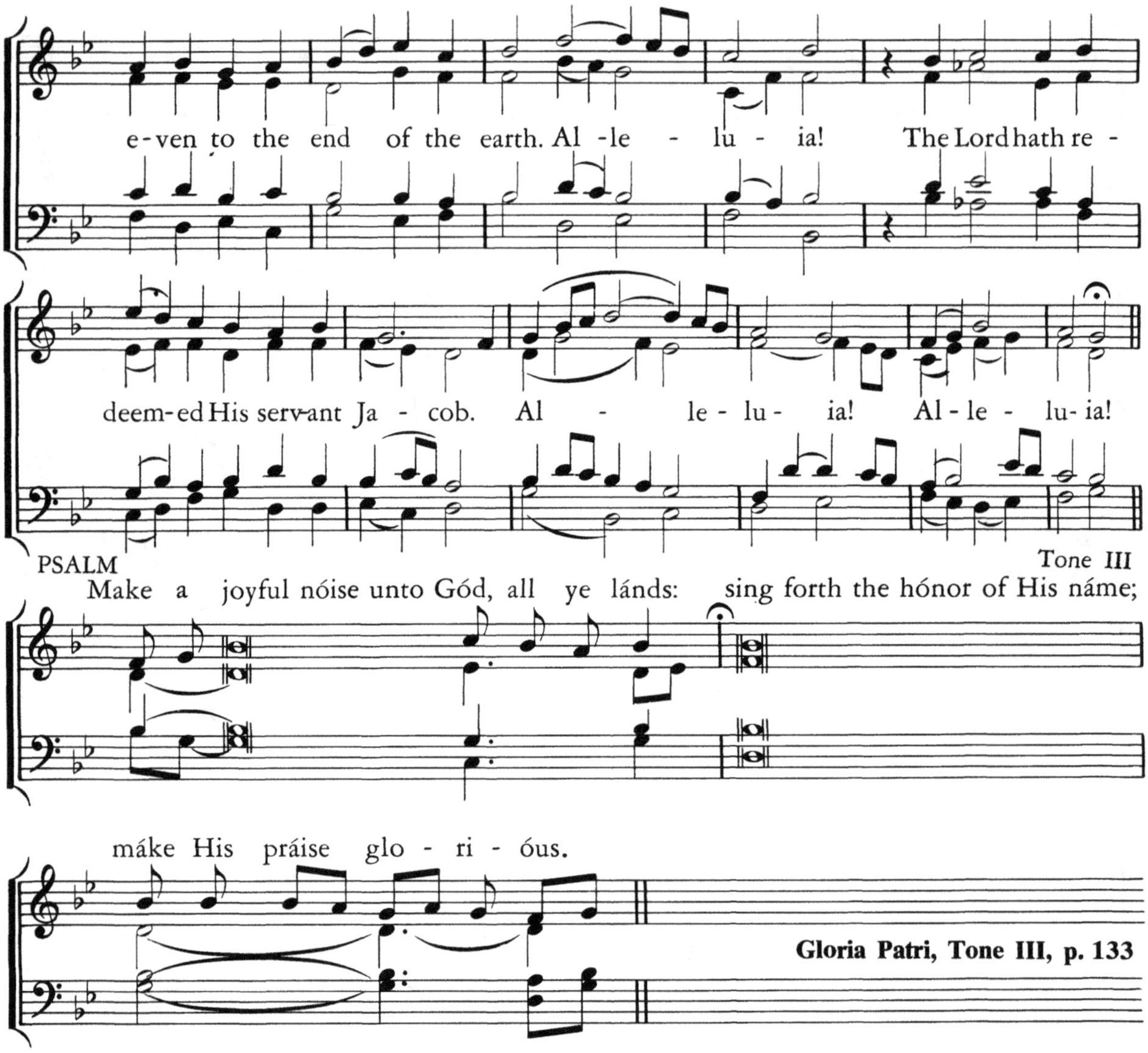

e-ven to the end of the earth. Al-le-lu-ia! The Lord hath re-
deem-ed His serv-ant Ja-cob. Al-le-lu-ia! Al-le-lu-ia!
PSALM
Tone III
Make a joyful nóise unto Gód, all ye lánds: sing forth the hónor of His náme;
máke His práise glo-ri-óus.
Gloria Patri, Tone III, p. 133

The Intervenient Chant
The Greater Alleluia

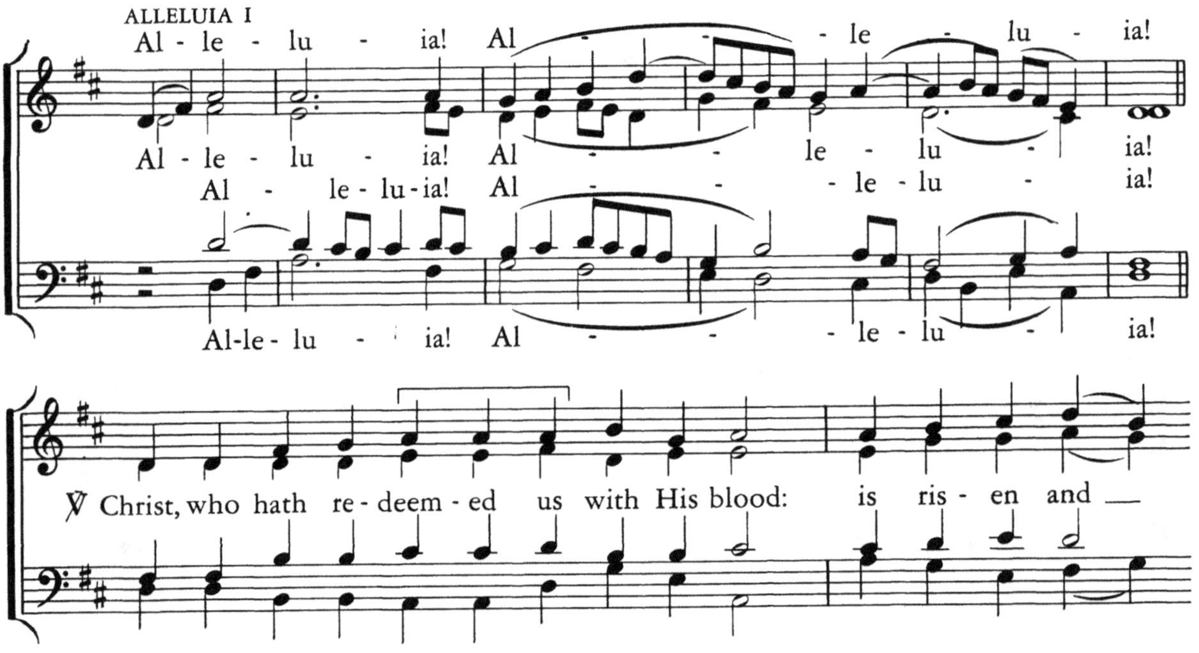

ALLELUIA I
Al-le-lu-ia! Al-le-lu-ia!
Al-le-lu-ia! Al-le-lu-ia!
Al-le-lu-ia! Al-le-lu-ia!
Al-le-lu-ia! Al-le-lu-ia!
℣ Christ, who hath re-deem-ed us with His blood: is ris-en and —

ALLELUIA II

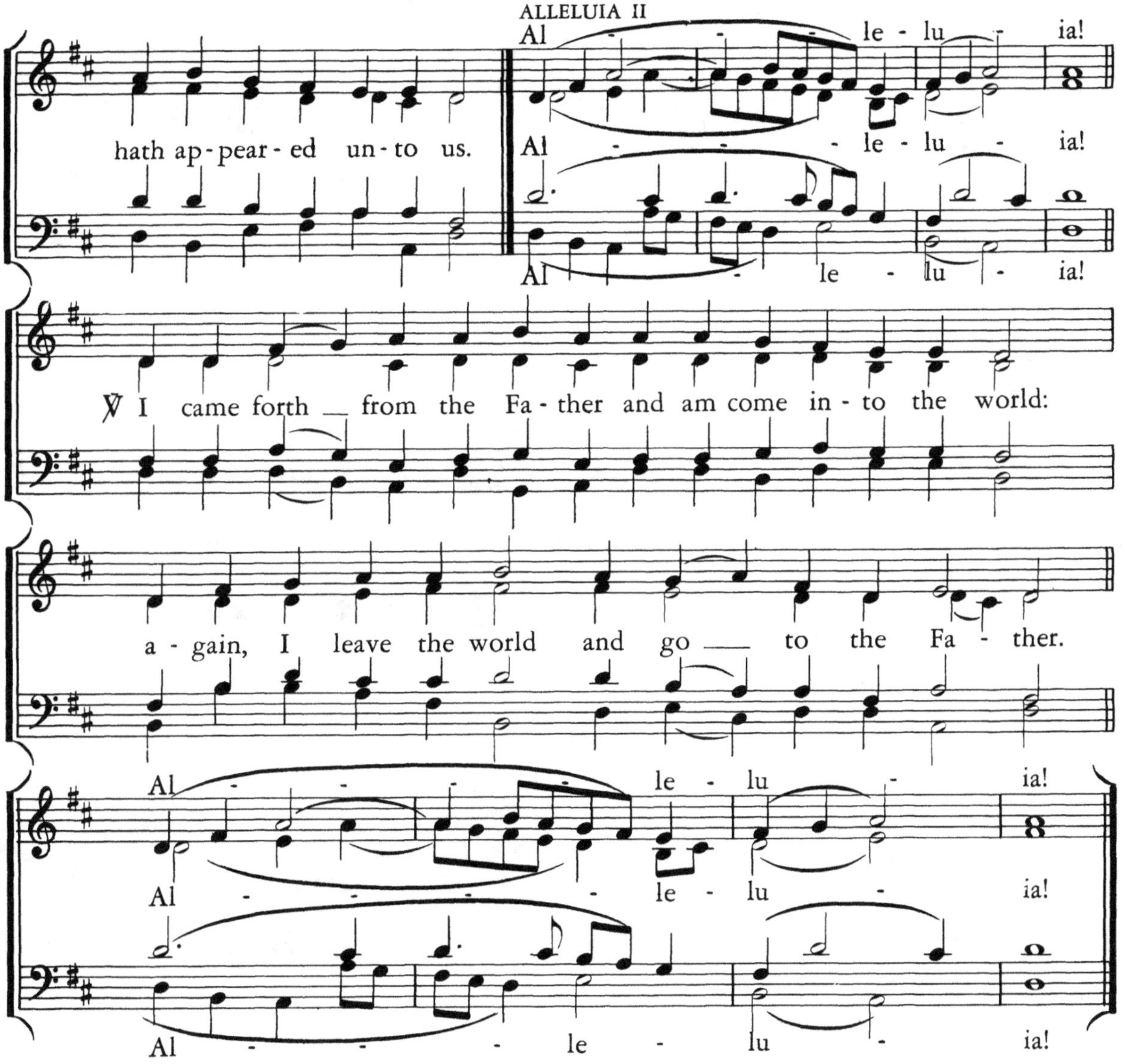

The Ascension of Our Lord

The Introit

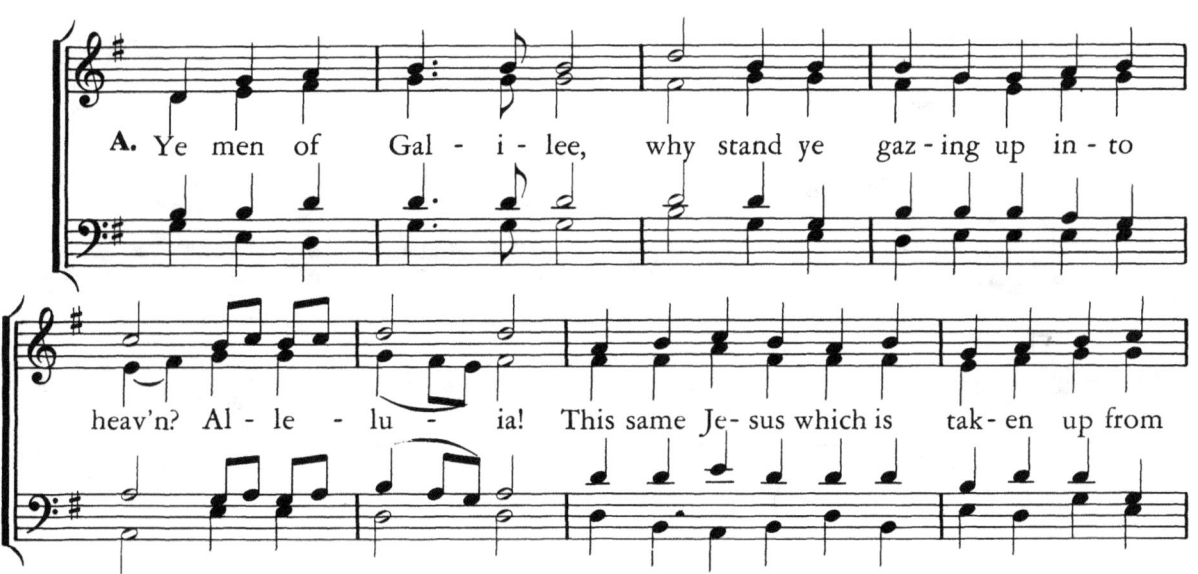

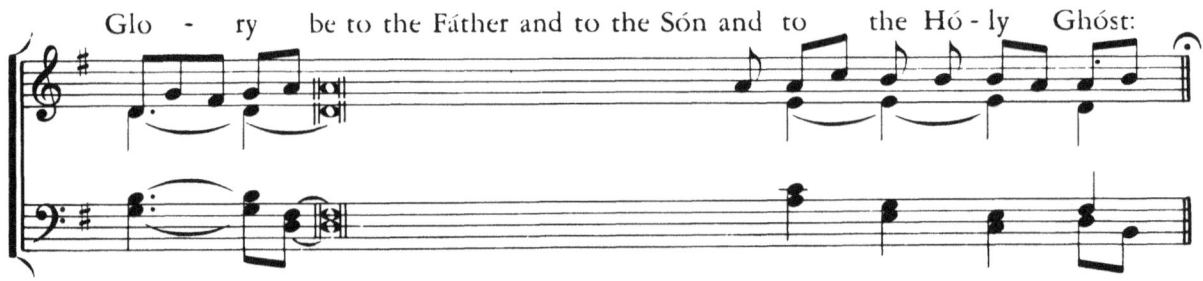

The Intervenient Chant
The Greater Alleluia

Exaudi, the Sunday After the Ascension

Gloria Patri, Tone I, p. 132

The Intervenient Chant
The Greater Alleluia

Whitsunday, the Feast of Pentecost

The Introit

A. The Spirit of the Lord filleth the world. Alleluia! Alleluia! Let the righteous be glad; let them rejoice before God; yea, let them exceedingly rejoice. Alleluia! Alleluia! Alleluia!

PSALM   Tone VIII

Let Gód aríse; let His én-e-mies be scattered: let them álso that háte Him flée beföre Him. Glóry be to the Fáther and to the Són and to the Hó-ly Ghost: as it wás in the beginning, is nów, and ev-er shálll be, wórld with-óut end. A-mén.

Repeat the Antiphon

The Intervenient Chant
The Greater Alleluia

The Feast of the Holy Trinity

The Introit

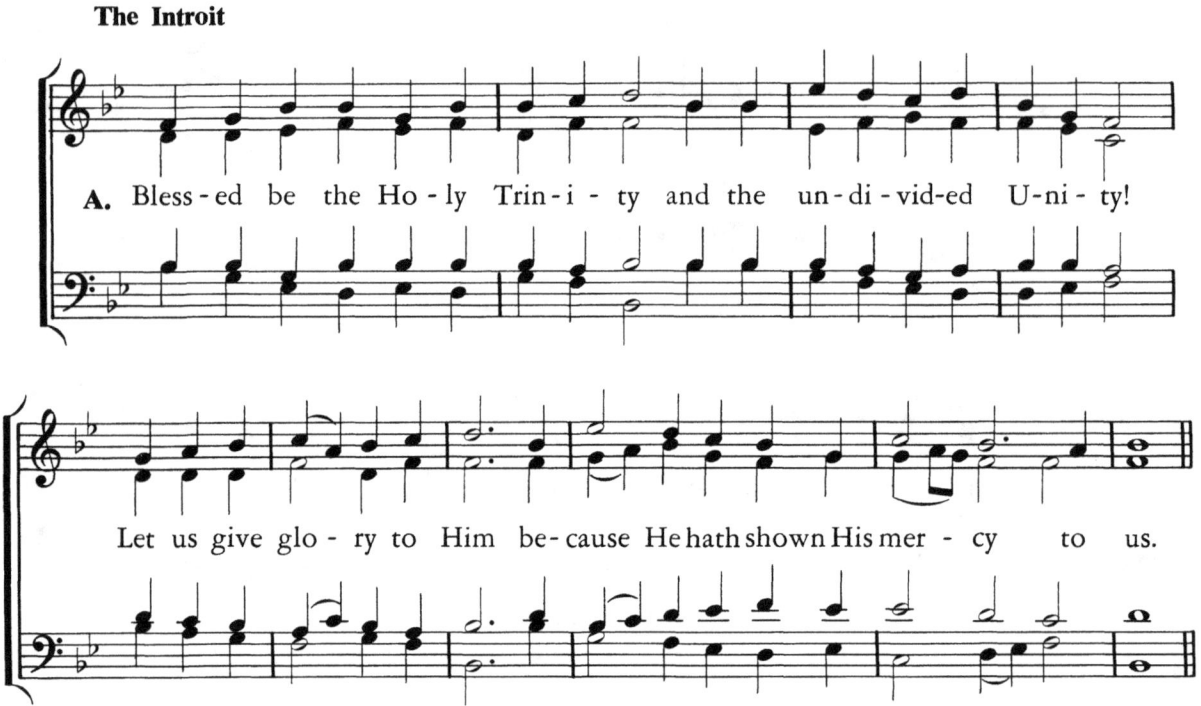

A. Blessed be the Holy Trinity and the undivided Unity! Let us give glory to Him because He hath shown His mercy to us.

PSALM   Tone VIII

O Lórd, our Lórd: how éx-cel-lent is Thy náme in all the earth!

Glo-ry be to the Fáther and to the Són and to the Hó-ly Ghost:

as it wás in the beginning, is nów, and ev-er shall be, wórld with-óut end. A-mén.

Repeat the Antiphon

The Intervenient Chants

THE GRADUAL

The First Sunday After Trinity

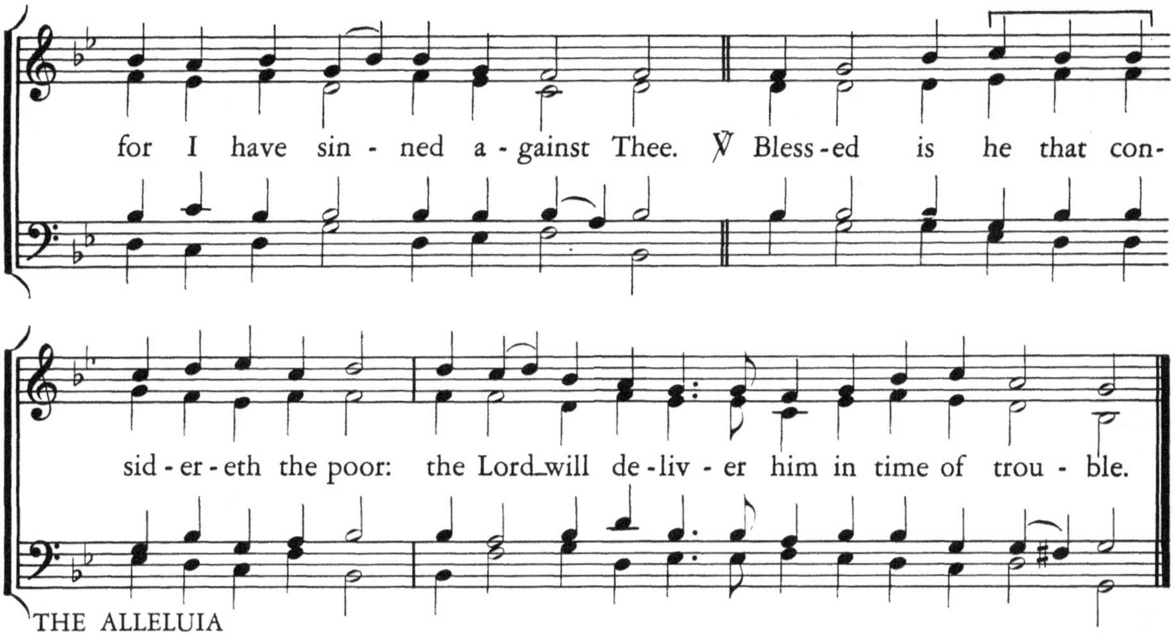

for I have sinned against Thee. ℣ Blessed is he that considereth the poor: the Lord will deliver him in time of trouble.

THE ALLELUIA

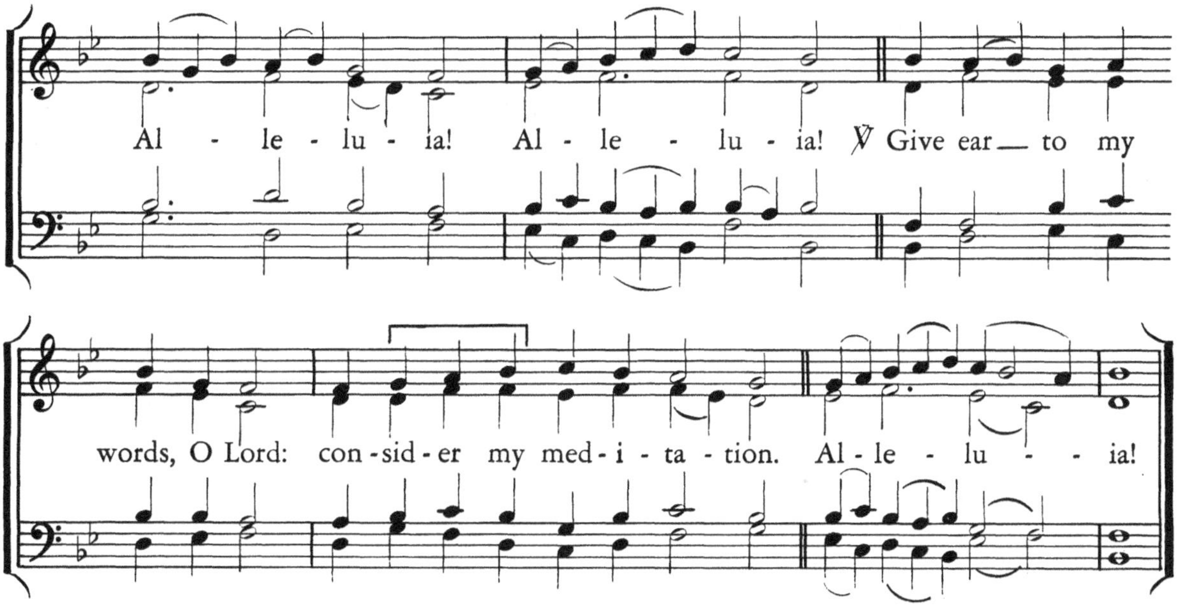

Alleluia! Alleluia! ℣ Give ear to my words, O Lord: consider my meditation. Alleluia!

The Second Sunday After Trinity

The Introit

A. The Lord was my Stay: He brought me forth

PSALM   TONE I

I will love Thee, O Lord, my Strength: The Lord is my Rock and my For-tress.

Gloria Patri, Tone I, p. 132

The Intervenient Chants

THE GRADUAL

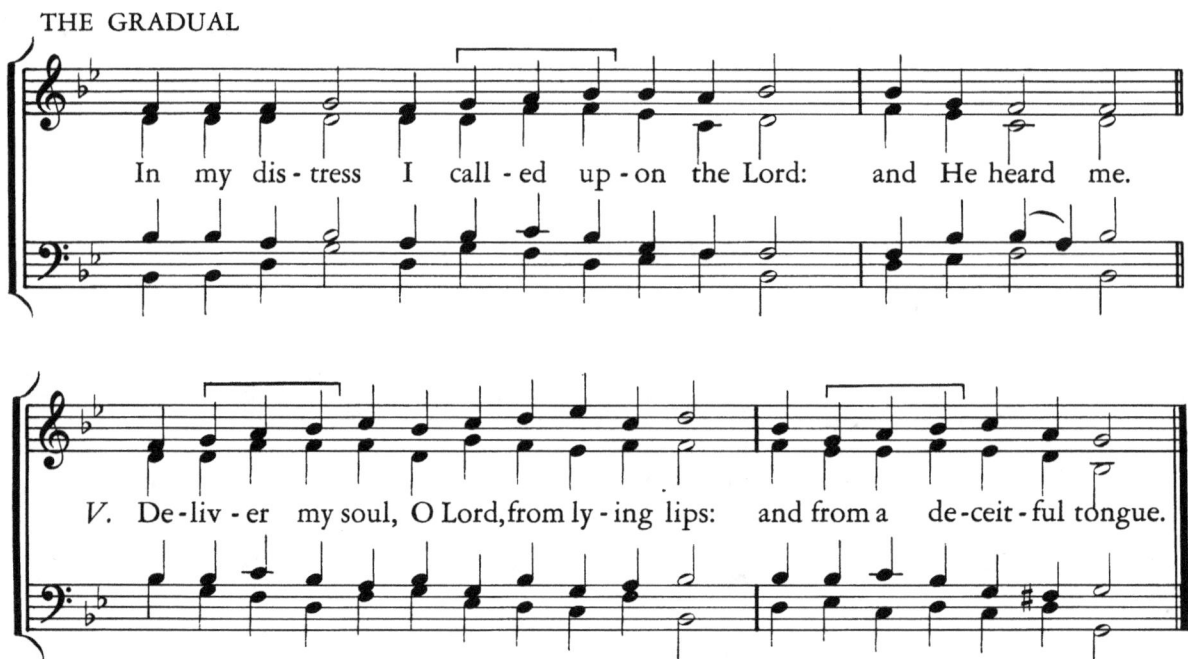

THE ALLELUIA

Alleluia! Alleluia! ℣ God judgeth the righteous: and God is angry with the wicked ev'ry day. Alleluia!

The Third Sunday After Trinity

The Introit

A. Turn Thee unto me and have mercy upon me: for I am desolate and afflicted. Look upon mine affliction and my pain: and forgive me all my sins.

PSALM

TONE VI

Gloria Patri, Tone VI, p. 134

The Intervenient Chants

THE GRADUAL

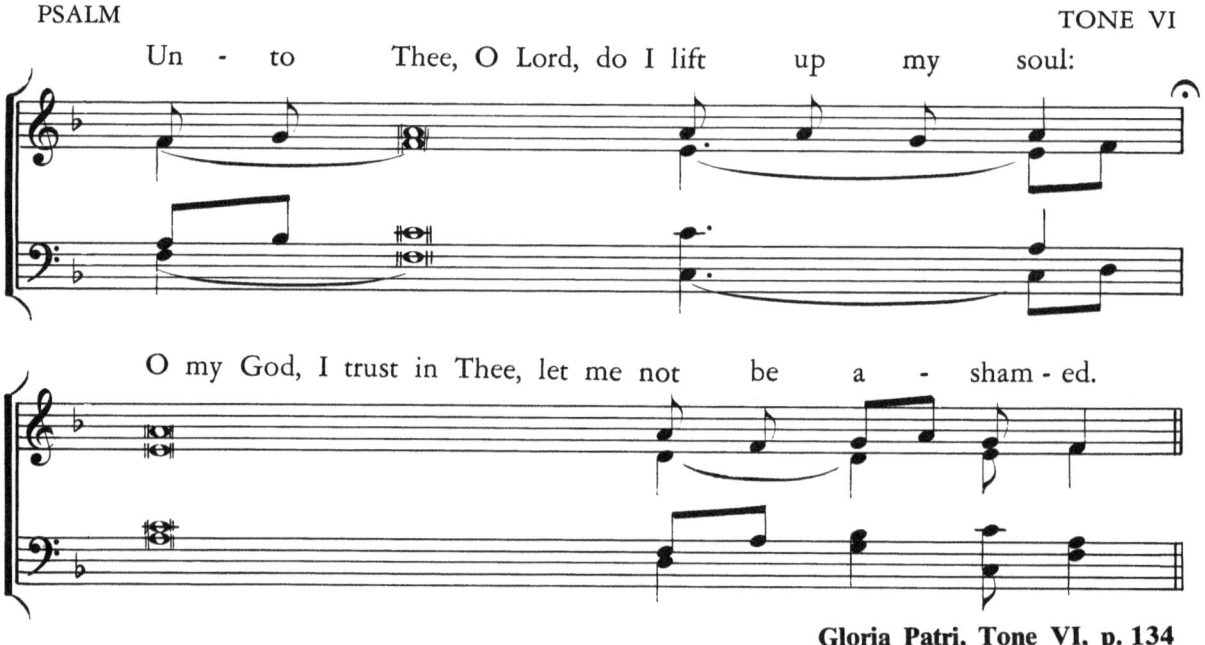

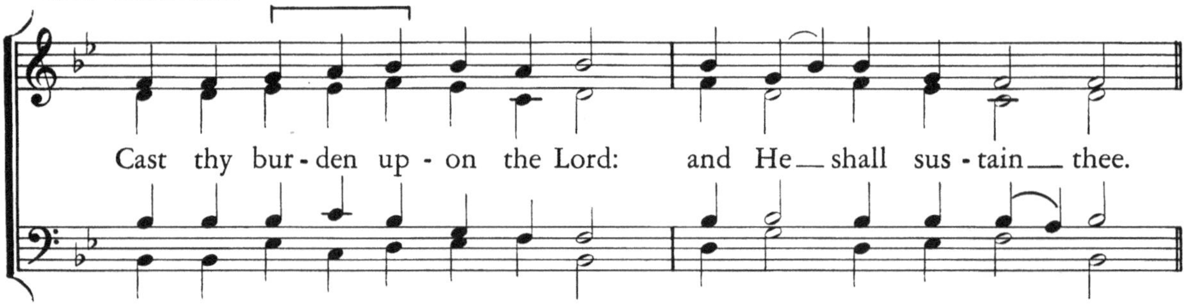

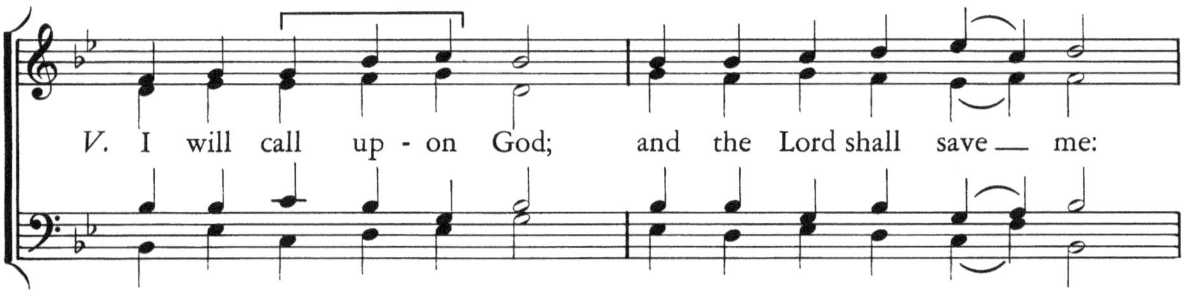

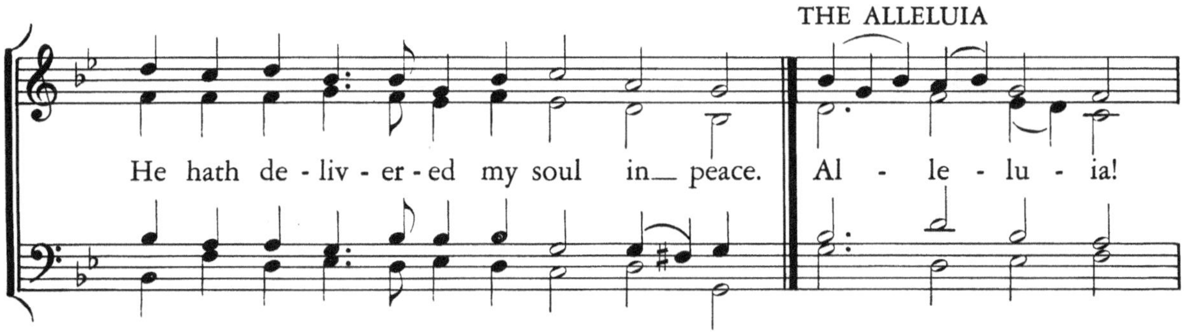

Alleluia! ℣ I will love Thee, O Lord, my Strength: the Lord is my Rock and my Fortress and my Deliverer. Alleluia!

The Fourth Sunday After Trinity

The Introit

A. The Lord is my Light and my Salvation; whom shall I fear?: The Lord is the Strength of my life; of whom shall I be afraid? When the wicked, even mine enemies and my foes, came up-on me: they stum-bled and fell.

PSALM TONE II

Though an host should encamp a-gainst me: my heart shall not fear.

Gloria Patri, Tone II, p. 132

The Intervenient Chants

THE GRADUAL

For-give our sins, O Lord: lest the hea-then say, Where is their God?

℣ Help us, O God of our sal-va-tion: and for the glo-ry of Thy name de-liv-er us.

THE ALLELUIA

Al - le - lu - ia! Al - le - lu - ia!

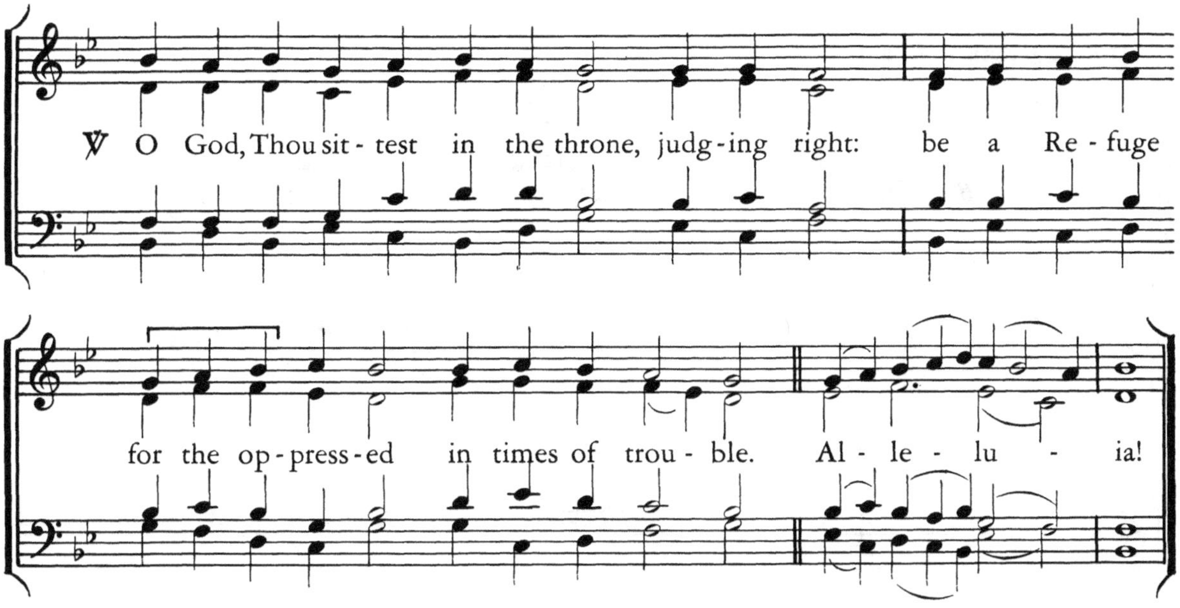

℣ O God, Thou sittest in the throne, judging right: be a Refuge for the oppressed in times of trouble. Alleluia!

The Fifth Sunday After Trinity

The Introit

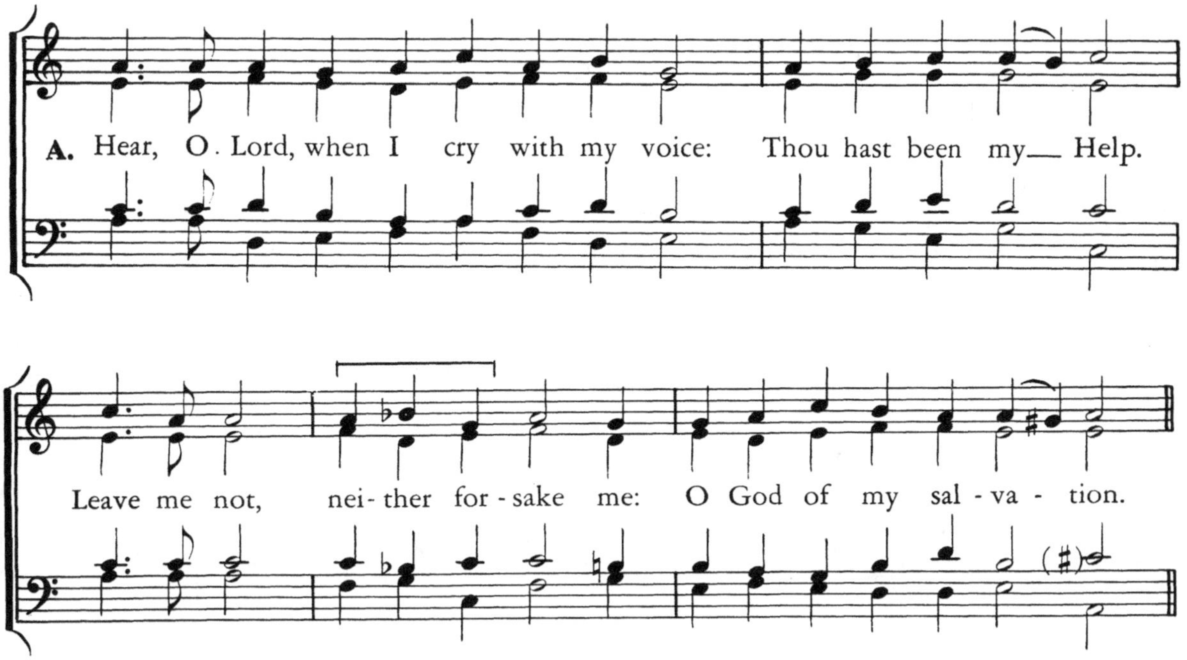

A. Hear, O Lord, when I cry with my voice: Thou hast been my Help. Leave me not, neither forsake me: O God of my salvation.

PSALM — TONE IV

The Lord is my Light and my Salvation: whom shall I fear?

Gloria Patri, Tone IV, p. 133

The Intervenient Chants

THE GRADUAL

Be-hold, O God, our Shield: and look up-on Thy ser-vants.

℣ O Lord God of hosts: hear our prayer.

THE ALLELUIA

Al - le - lu - ia! Al - le - lu - ia! ℣ The king shall joy in Thy strength: and in Thy sal-vation, how great-ly shall he re-joice! Al - le - lu - ia!

The Sixth Sunday After Trinity

The Introit

A. The Lord is the Strength of His peo-ple: He is the sav-

PSALM — TONE II

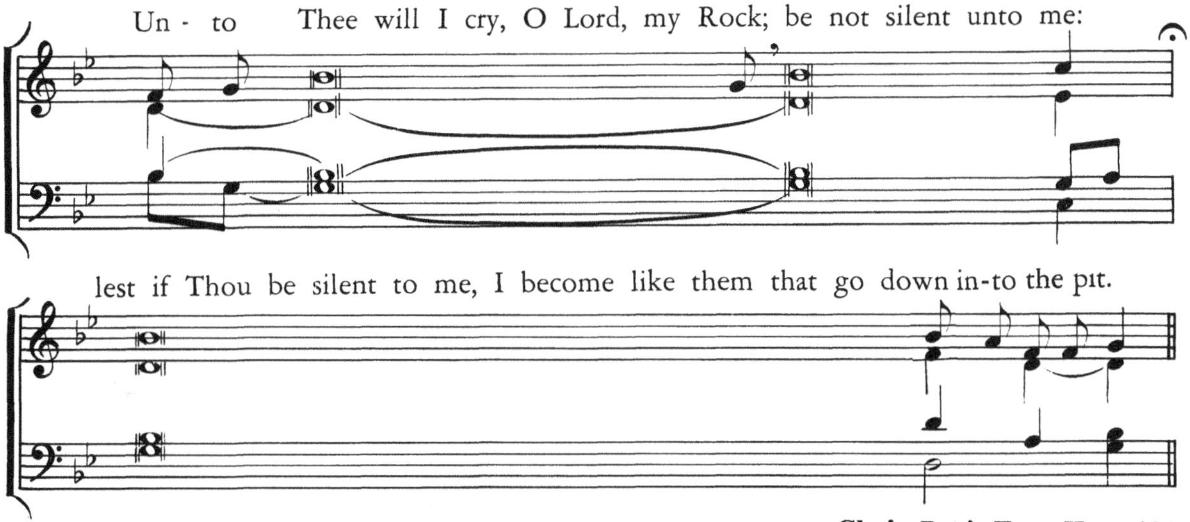

ing Strength of His anointed. Save Thy people and bless Thine inheritance: feed them also and lift them up forever.

Unto Thee will I cry, O Lord, my Rock; be not silent unto me: lest if Thou be silent to me, I become like them that go down into the pit.

Gloria Patri, Tone II, p. 132

The Intervenient Chants

THE GRADUAL

Return, O Lord, how long?: and let it repent Thee concerning Thy servants.

℣ Lord, Thou hast been our Dwelling place in all generations.

THE ALLELUIA

Alleluia! Alleluia! ℣ In Thee, O Lord, do I put my trust; let me never be ashamed: deliver me in Thy righteousness: bow down Thine ear to me, deliver me speedily. Alleluia!

The Seventh Sunday After Trinity

The Introit

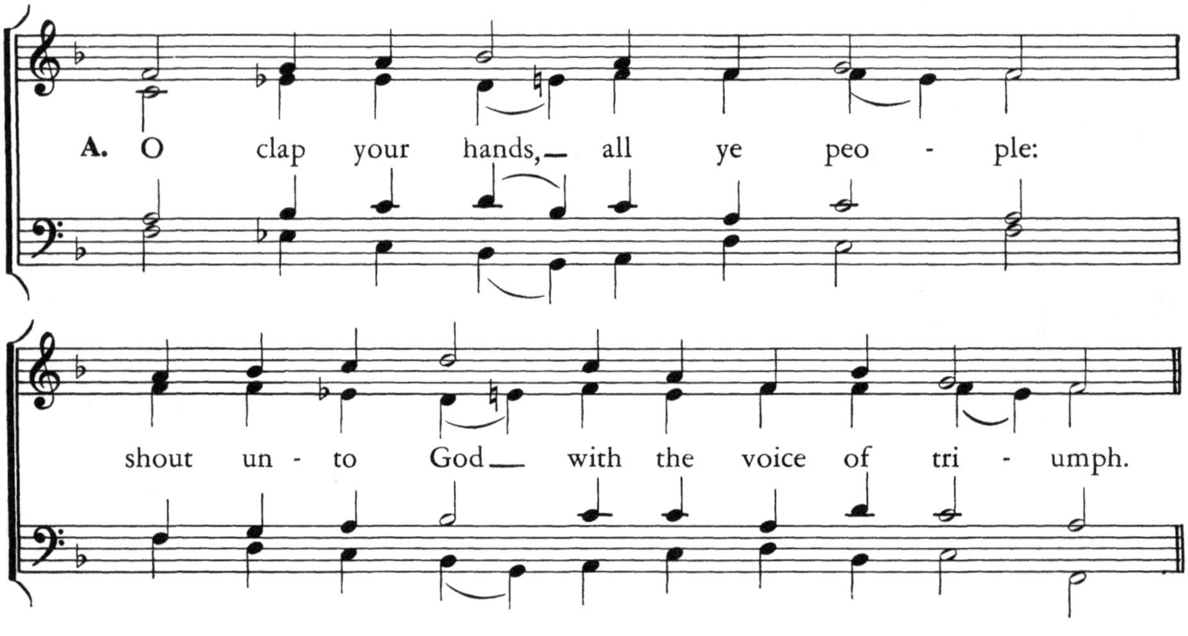

A. O clap your hands, all ye people: shout unto God with the voice of triumph.

The Eighth Sunday After Trinity

The Introit

A. We have thought of Thy loving-kindness, O God: in the midst of Thy temple. According to Thy name, O God, so is Thy praise unto the ends of the earth: Thy right hand is full of righteousness.

PSALM — TONE I

Great is the Lord, and greatly to be praised: in the city of our God, in the mountain of His holiness.

Gloria Patri, Tone I, p. 132

The Intervenient Chants

The Ninth Sunday After Trinity

The Introit

A. Be-hold, God is mine Help-er: The Lord is with them that up-hold my soul. He shall re-ward e-vil un-to mine en-e-mies: cut them off in Thy truth, O Lord.

PSALM   TONE V

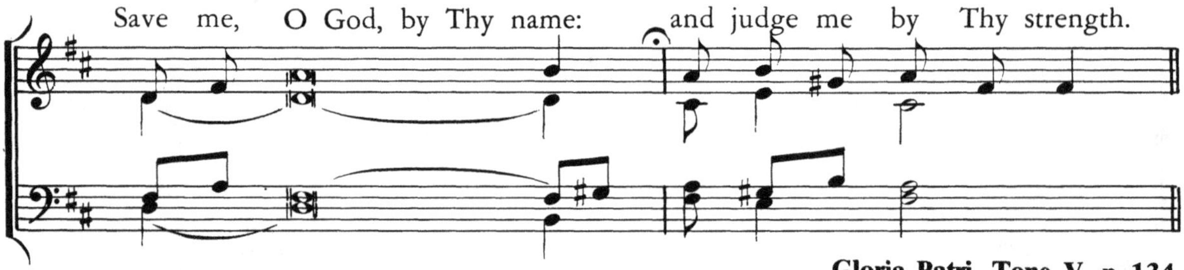

Save me, O God, by Thy name: and judge me by Thy strength.

Gloria Patri, Tone V, p. 134

The Intervenient Chants

THE GRADUAL

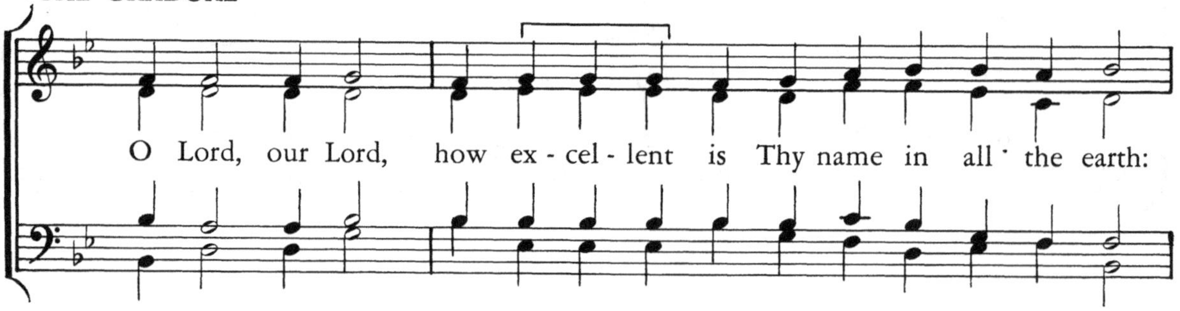

O Lord, our Lord, how ex-cel-lent is Thy name in all the earth:

THE ALLELUIA

The Tenth Sunday After Trinity

The Introit

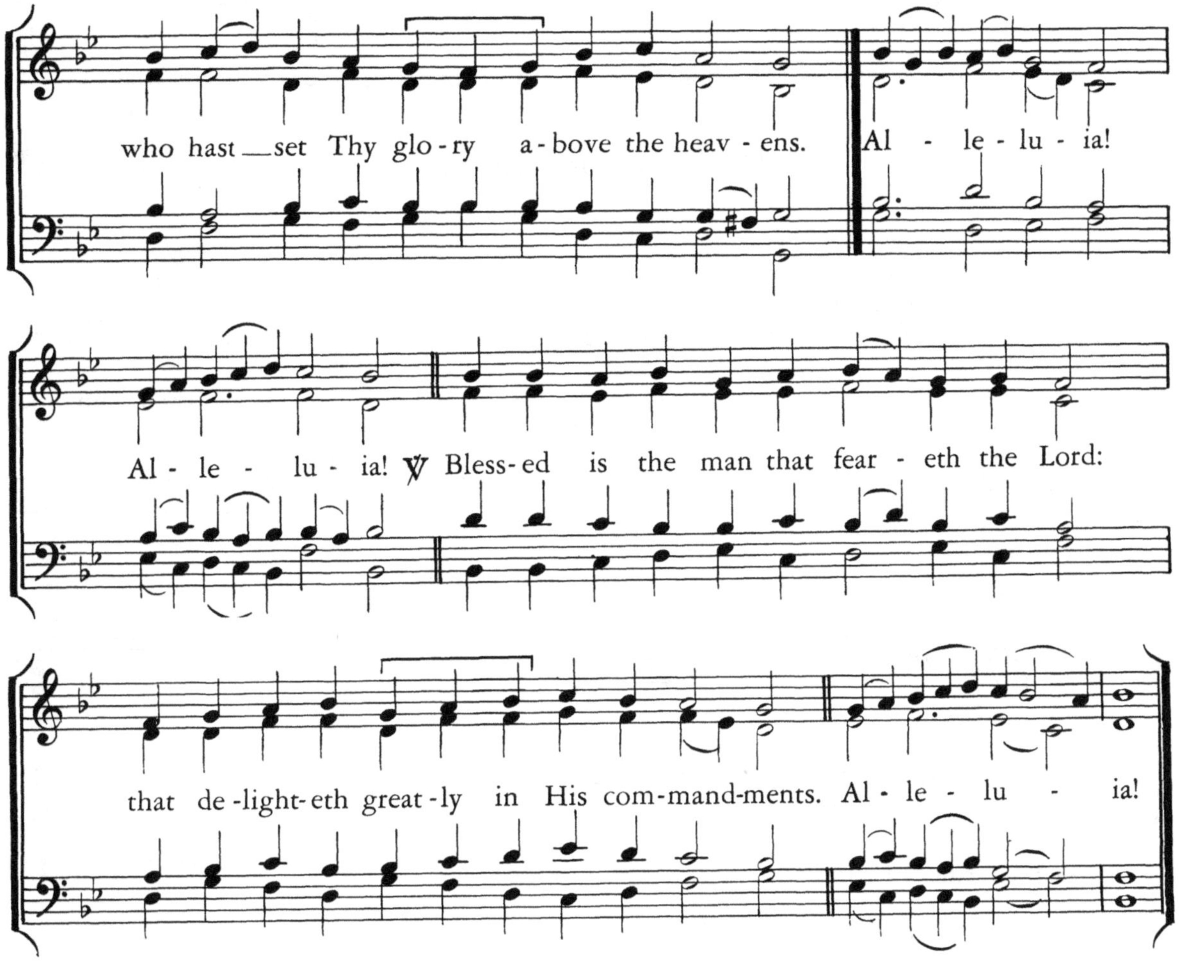

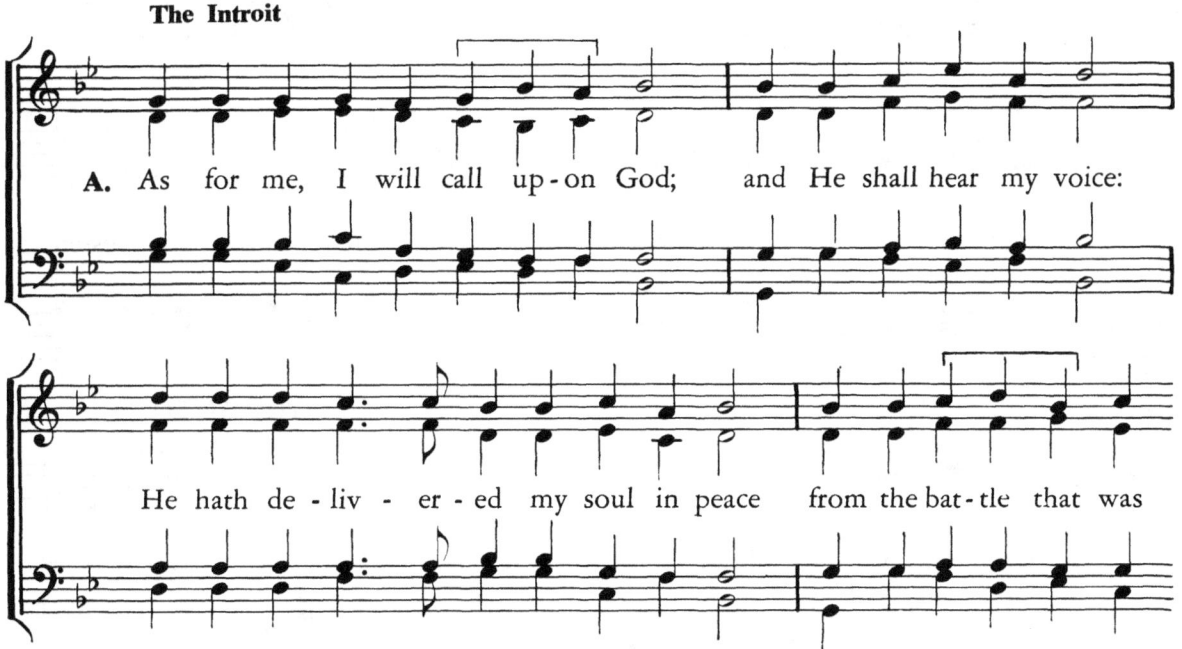

Alleluia! ℣ O Lord God of my salvation, I have cried day and night before Thee. Alleluia!

The Eleventh Sunday After Trinity

The Introit

A. God is in His holy habitation: He is God who setteth the solitary in families. The God of Israel is He that giveth strength: and pow'r unto His people.

Gloria Patri, Tone V, p. 134

The Intervenient Chants

THE GRADUAL

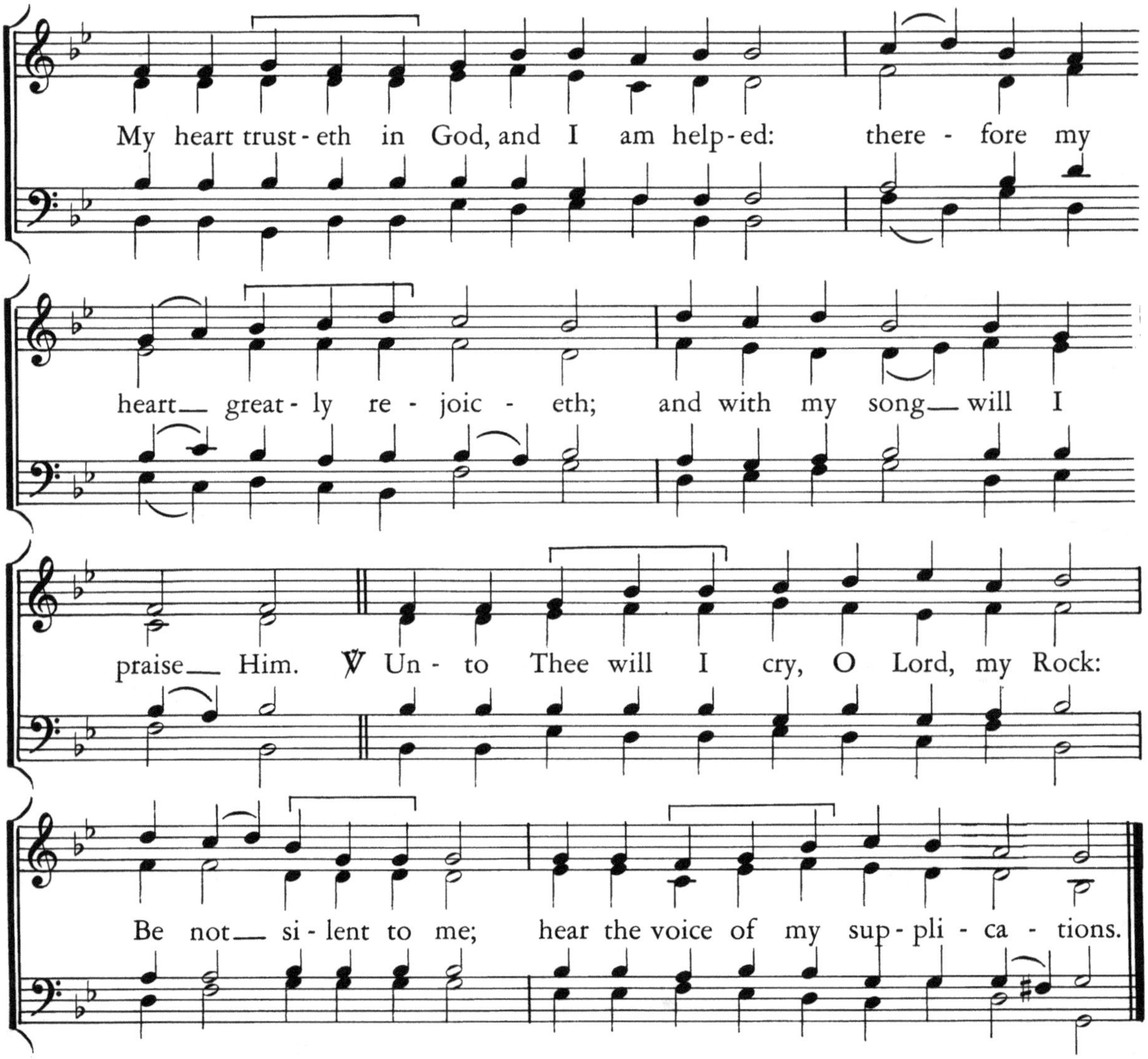

THE ALLELUIA

The Twelfth Sunday After Trinity

The Introit

PSALM   TONE VII

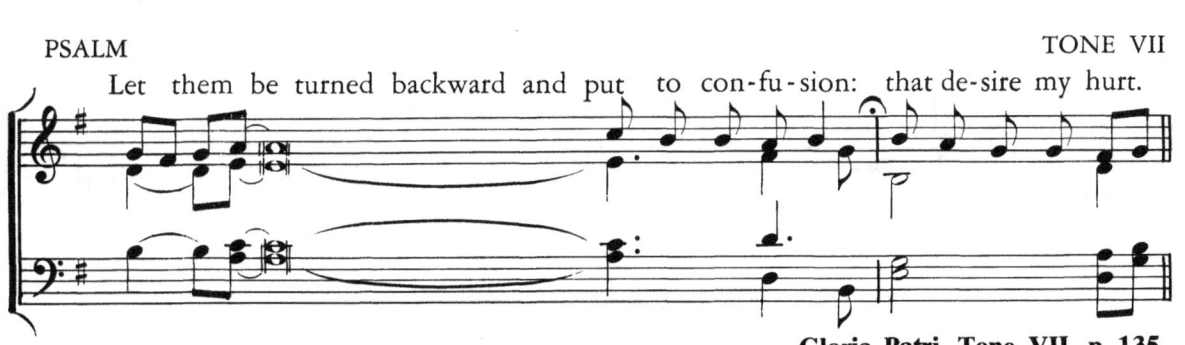

Gloria Patri, Tone VII, p. 135

The Intervenient Chants

The Thirteenth Sunday After Trinity

The Introit

A. Have respect, O Lord, unto Thy covenant: O let not the oppressed return ashamed. Arise, O God, plead Thine own cause: and forget not the voice of Thine enemies.

PSALM TONE VII

O God, why hast Thou cast us off forever?: Why doth Thine anger smoke against the sheep of Thy pasture?

Gloria Patri, Tone VII, p. 135

The Intervenient Chants

THE GRADUAL

THE ALLELUIA

The Fourteenth Sunday After Trinity

The Introit

A. Behold, O God, our Shield, and look upon the face of Thine a-

nointed; for a day in Thy courts is better than a thousand.

PSALM   TONE IV
How á-miable are Thy tábernacles, O Lórd of hósts: My soul lóngeth, yea, even

fáinteth for the cóurts of the Lórd.

Gloria Patri, Tone IV, p. 133

The Intervenient Chants

THE GRADUAL

It is a good thing to give thanks unto the Lord: and to sing praises un-to Thy name, O Most High, ℣ To show forth Thy lov-ing-kind-ness

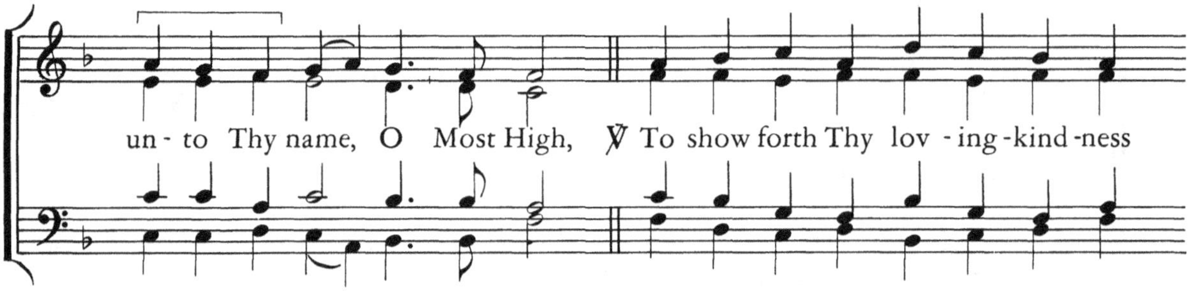

THE ALLELUIA

in the morn-ing: and Thy faith-ful-ness ev-'ry night. Al-le-lu-ia!

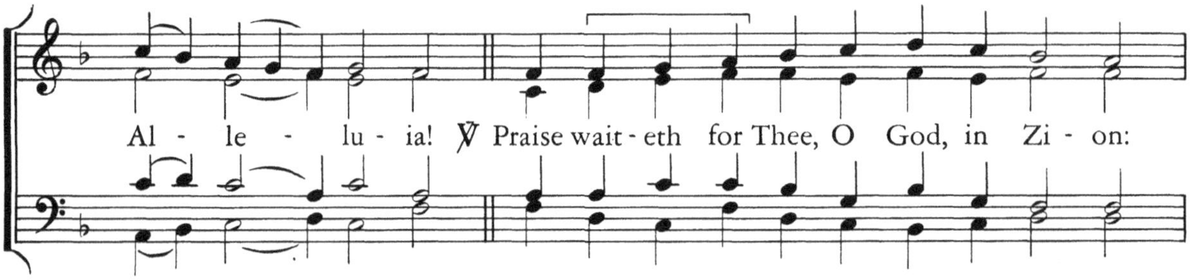

Al-le-lu-ia! ℣ Praise wait-eth for Thee, O God, in Zi-on:

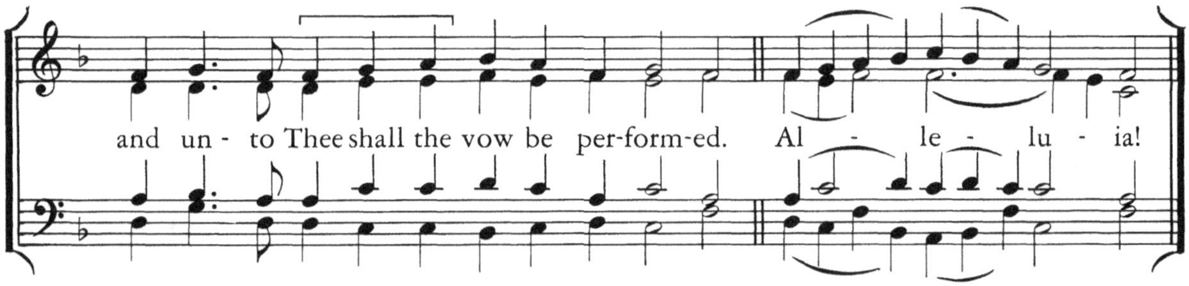

and un-to Thee shall the vow be per-form-ed. Al-le-lu-ia!

The Fifteenth Sunday After Trinity

The Introit

A. Bow down Thine ear, O Lord, hear me: O Thou, my God,

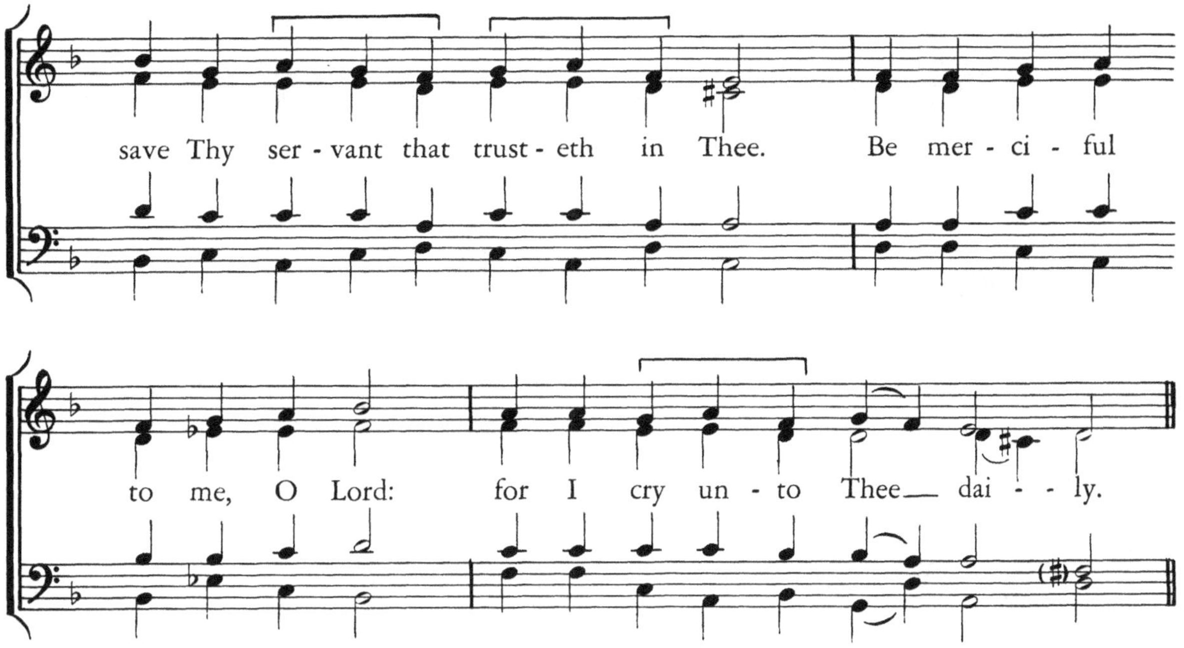

PSALM TONE I

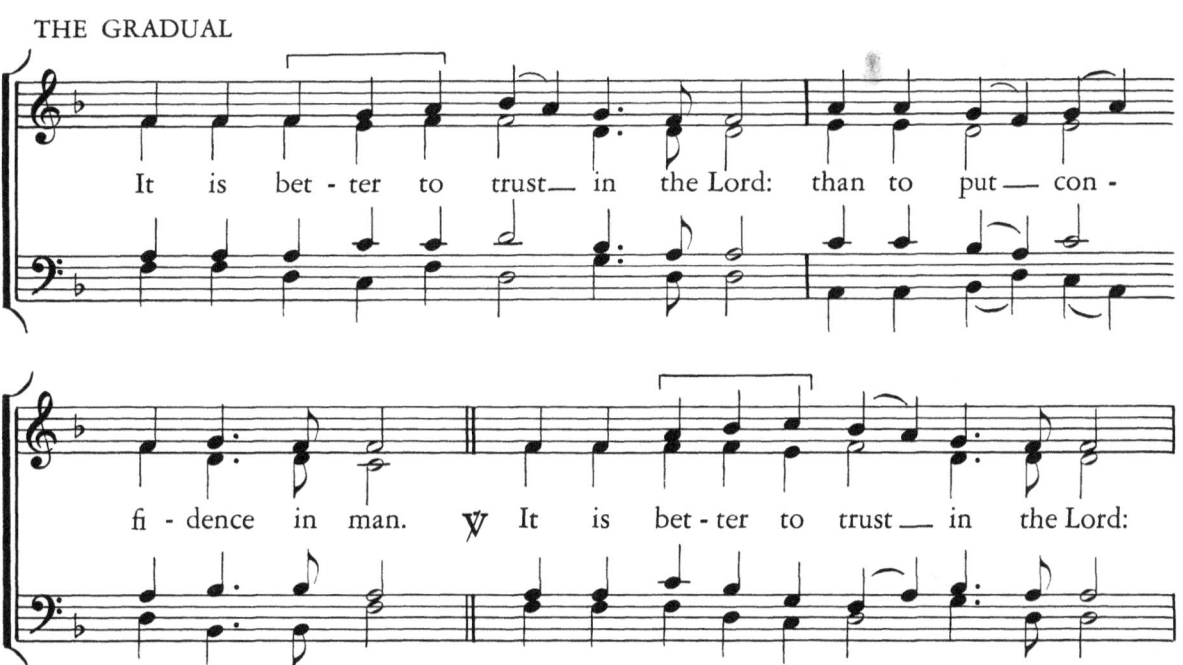

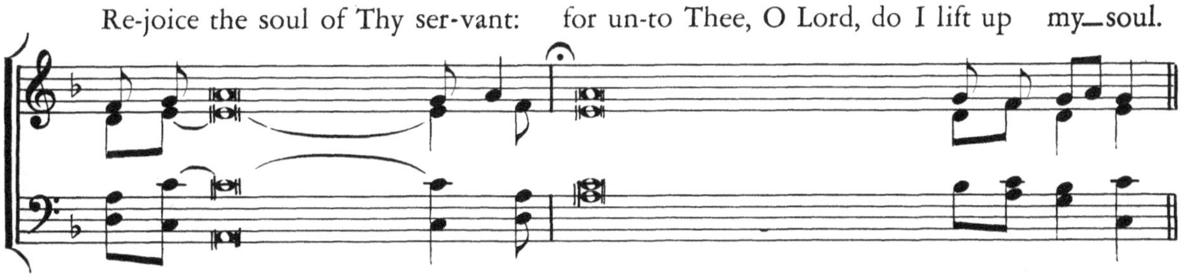

Gloria Patri, Tone I, p. 132

The Intervenient Chants

THE GRADUAL

THE ALLELUIA

than to put confidence in princes. Alleluia! Alleluia! ℣ O God, my heart is fixed: I will sing and give praise, even with my glory. Alleluia!

The Sixteenth Sunday After Trinity

The Introit

A. Be merciful unto me, O Lord: for I cry unto Thee daily. For Thou, Lord, art good and ready to forgive:

and plen - te - ous in mer - cy un - to all them that call up - on Thee.

PSALM　　　　　　　　　　　　　　　　　　　　　　　　　　　　　TONE VIII

Bow down Thine ear, O Lord, hear me:　　for I am poor and need - y.

Gloria Patri, Tone VIII, p. 135

The Intervenient Chants

THE GRADUAL

The hea - then shall fear the name— of the Lord: and all the kings of the earth Thy glo - ry. ℣ When the Lord shall build up Zi - on:

THE ALLELUIA

He shall ap - pear— in — His glo - ry　Al - le - lu - ia!

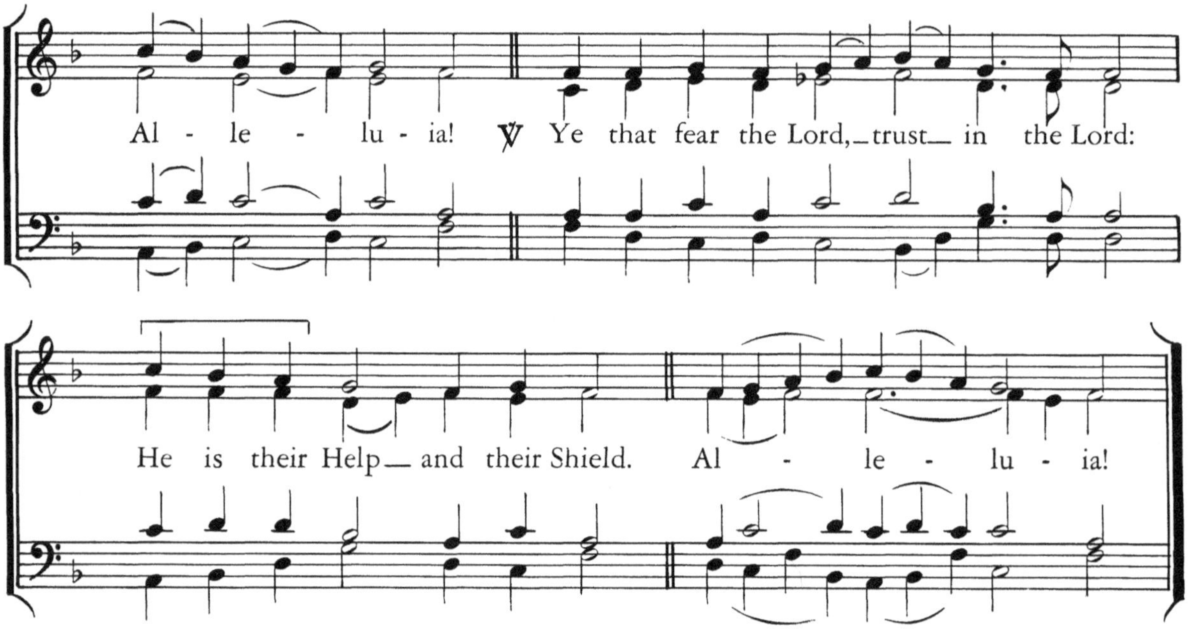

The Seventeenth Sunday After Trinity

The Introit

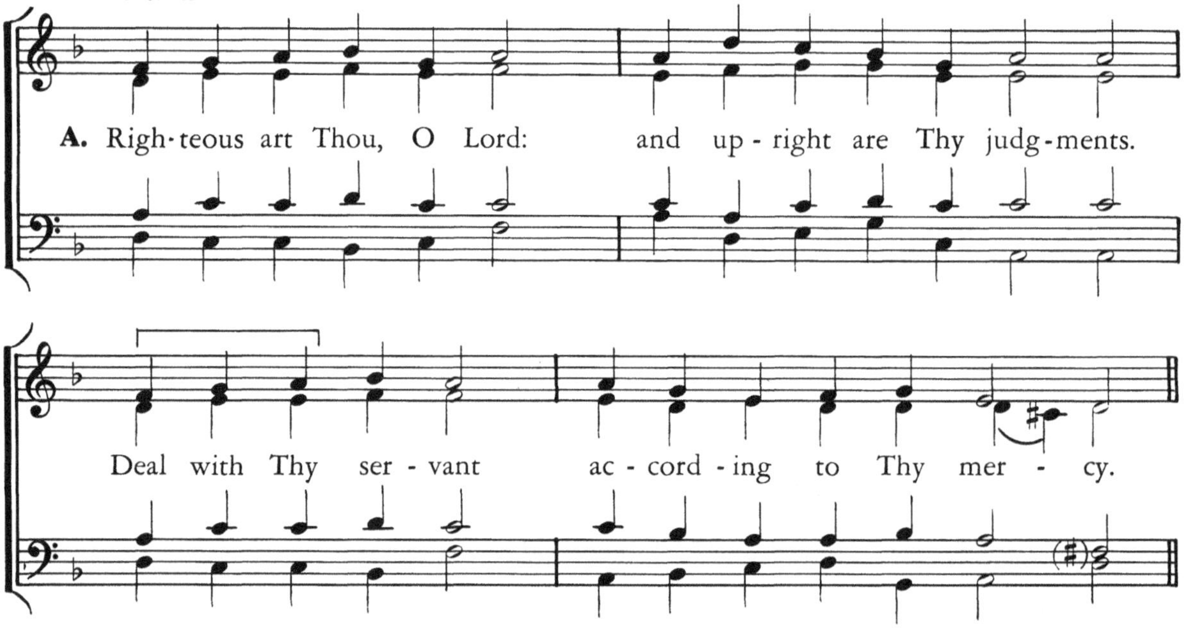

PSALM TONE I

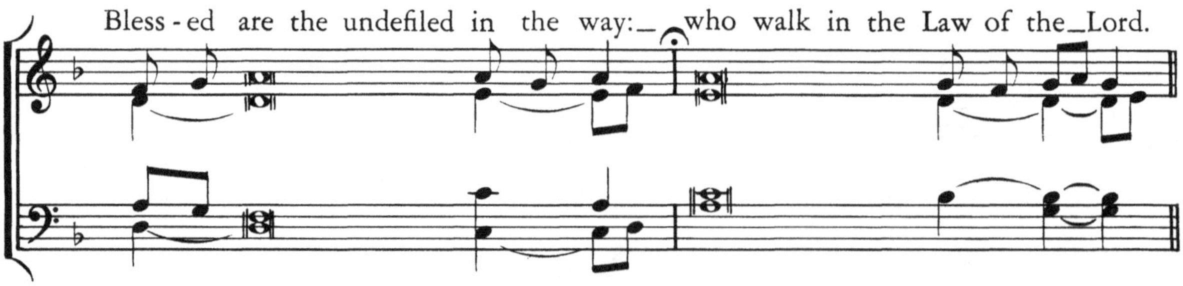

Gloria Patri, Tone I, p. 132

The Intervenient Chants

THE GRADUAL

THE ALLELUIA

-per-i-ty with-in thy pal-a-ces: Al-le-lu-ia! Al-le-lu-ia! ℣ O praise the Lord, all ye na-tions: praise Him, all ye peo-ple. Al-le-lu-ia!

The Nineteenth Sunday After Trinity

The Introit

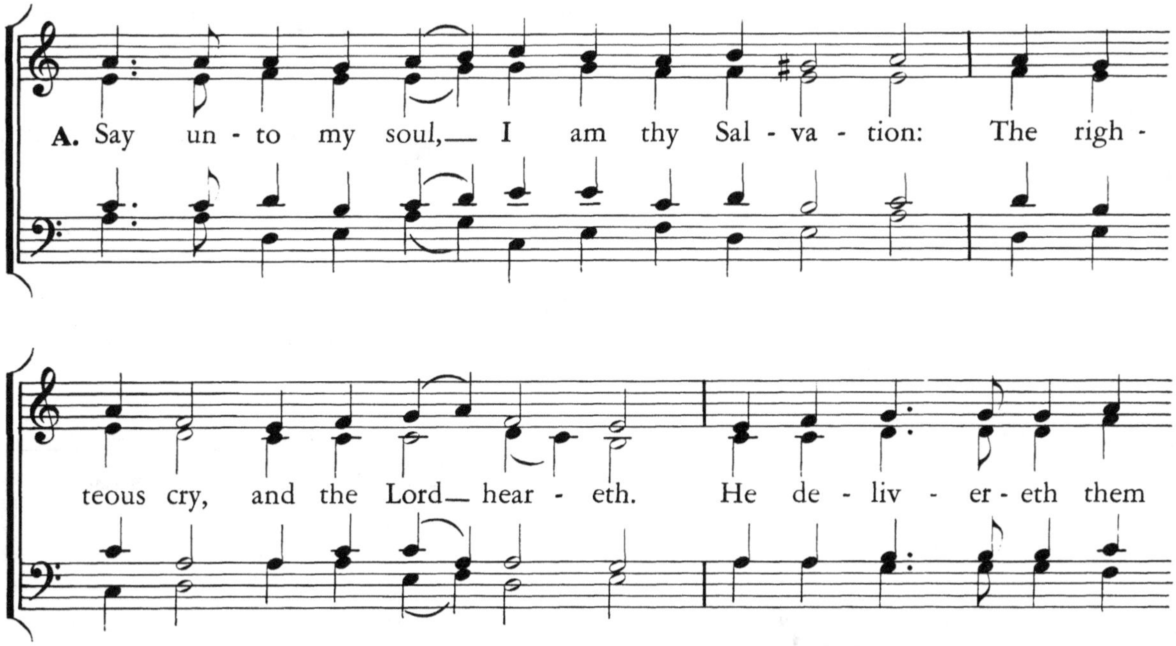

A. Say un-to my soul, I am thy Sal-va-tion: The righ-teous cry, and the Lord hear-eth. He de-liv-er-eth them

The Twentieth Sunday After Trinity

The Introit

A. The Lord, our God, is righteous in all His works which He doeth: for we obeyed not His voice. Give glory to Thy name, O Lord: and deal with us according to the multitude of Thy mercies.

PSALM — TONE III

Great is the Lord and greatly to be praised: in the city of our God, in the mountain of His holiness.

Gloria Patri, Tone III, p. 133

The Intervenient Chants

THE GRADUAL

The Twenty-first Sunday After Trinity

The Introit

A. The whole world is in Thy power, O Lord, King Almighty; there is no man that can gainsay Thee. For Thou hast made heav'n and earth and all the wondrous things under the heav'n; Thou art Lord of all.

PSALM   Tone IV

Blessed are the undefiled in the way: who walk in the Law of the Lord.

Gloria Patri, Tone IV, p. 133

The Intervenient Chants

THE GRADUAL

Lord, Thou hast been our Dwelling Place: in all generations.

118

℣ Before the mountains were brought forth or ever Thou hadst formed the earth and the world: even from everlasting to everlasting Thou art God.

THE ALLELUIA

Alleluia! Alleluia!

℣ They that trust in the Lord shall be as Mount Zion: which cannot be removed, but abideth forever. Alleluia!

The Twenty-second Sunday After Trinity

The Introit

A. If Thou, Lord, shouldest mark iniquities:

O Lord, _ who shall stand? But there is for-give-ness with Thee: that Thou may-est be fear-ed: O God of _ Is-ra-el.

PSALM TONE III

Out of the depths here have I cried un-to Thee, O Lord: Lord, hear my voice. _

Gloria Patri, Tone III, p. 133

The Intervenient Chants

THE GRADUAL

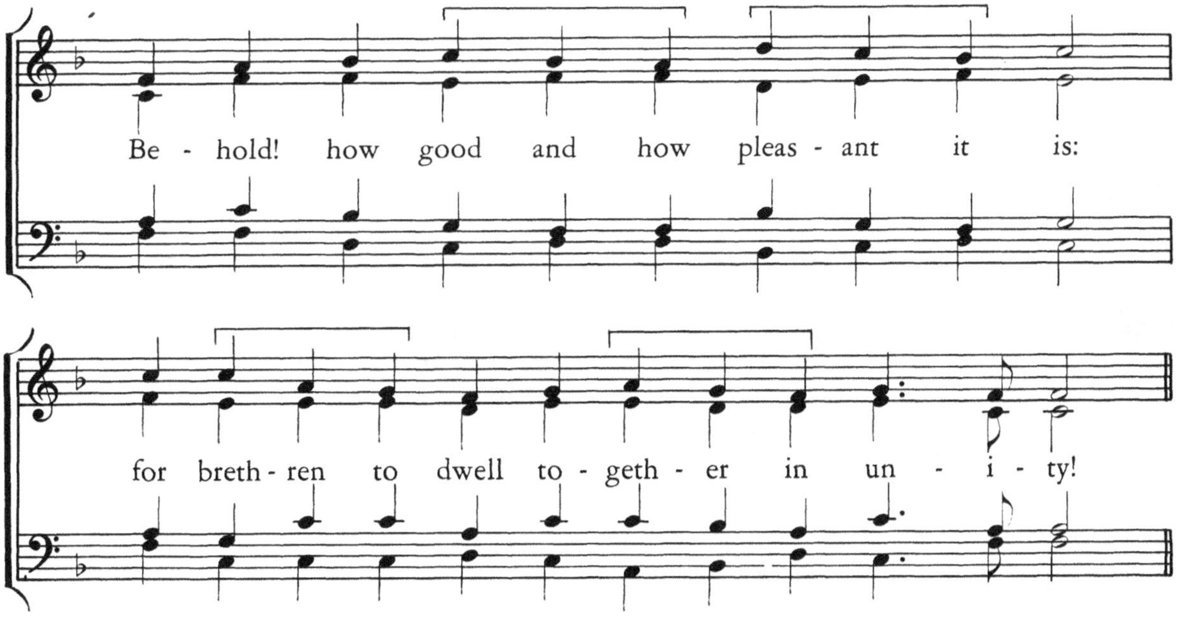

Be-hold! how good and how pleas-ant it is: for breth-ren to dwell to-geth-er in un-i-ty!

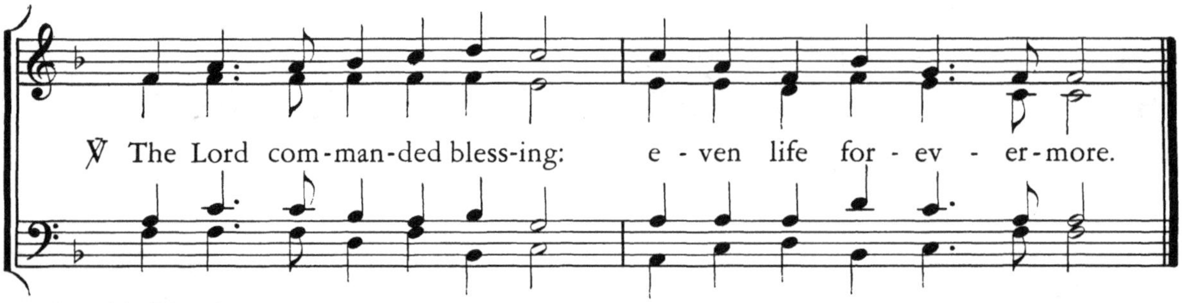
℣ The Lord com-man-ded bless-ing: e - ven life for - ev - er-more.

THE ALLELUIA

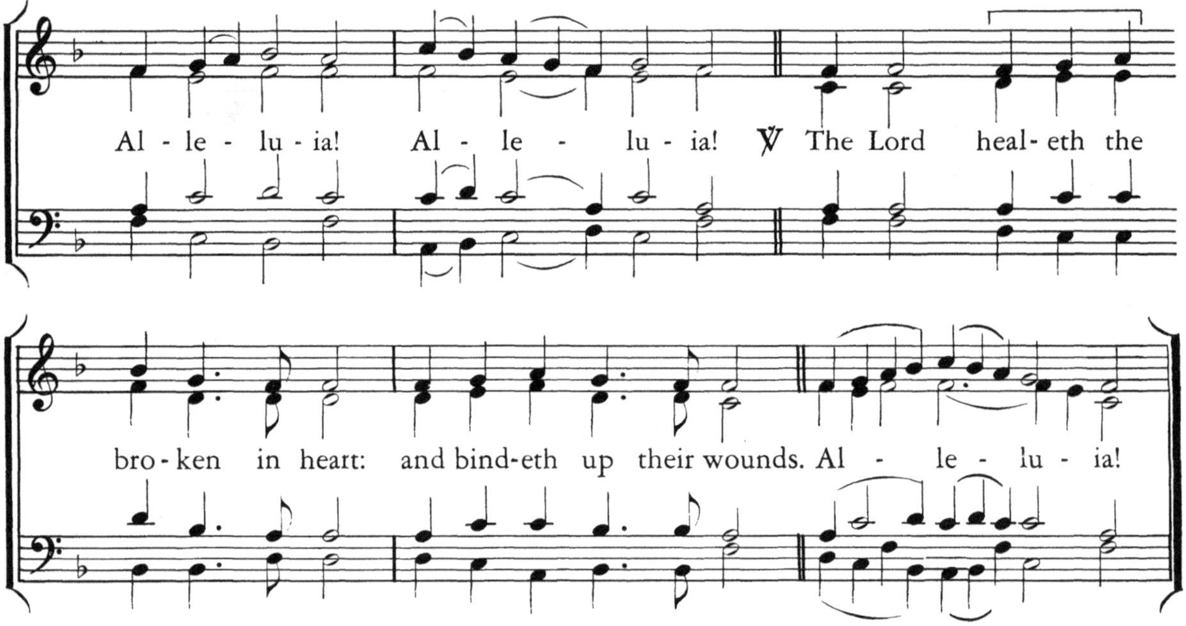
Al - le - lu - ia! Al - le - lu - ia! ℣ The Lord heal-eth the
bro-ken in heart: and bind-eth up their wounds. Al - le - lu - ia!

The Twenty-third Sunday After Trinity

The Introit

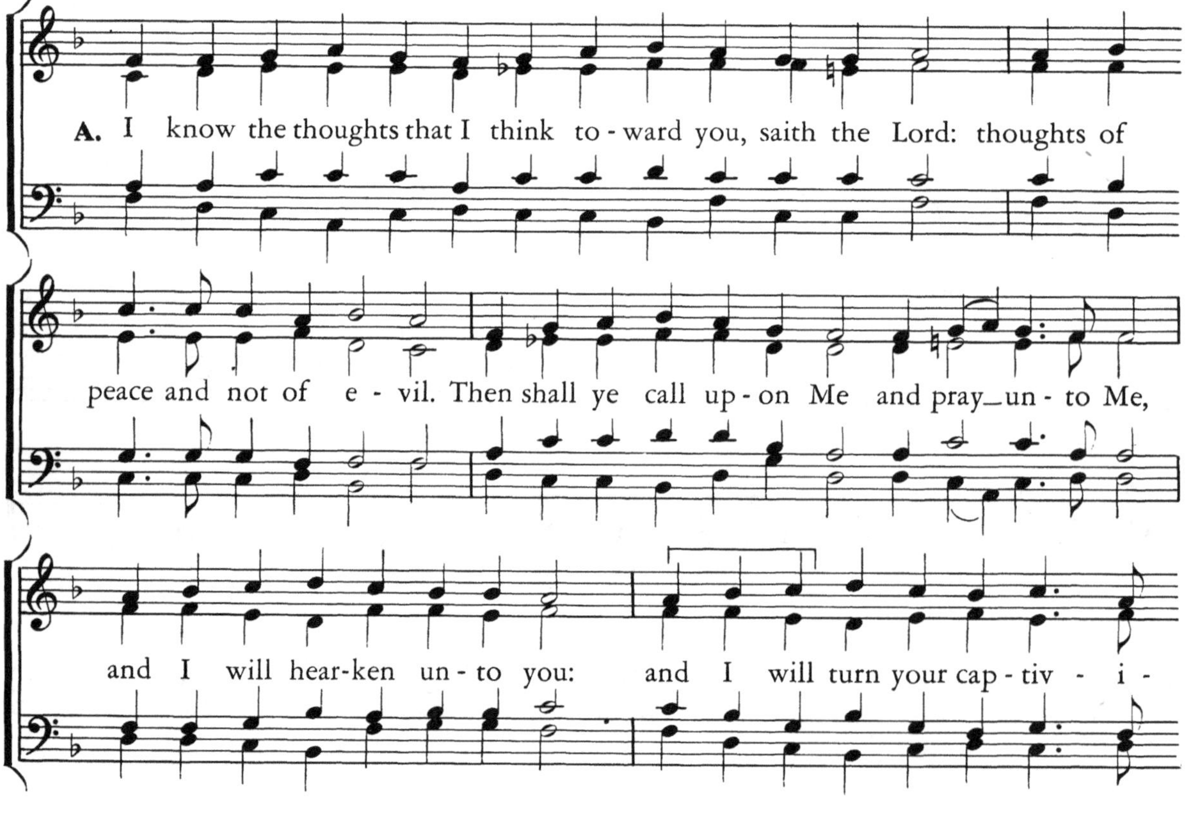
A. I know the thoughts that I think to-ward you, saith the Lord: thoughts of
peace and not of e - vil. Then shall ye call up-on Me and pray_un - to Me,
and I will hear-ken un - to you: and I will turn your cap - tiv - i -

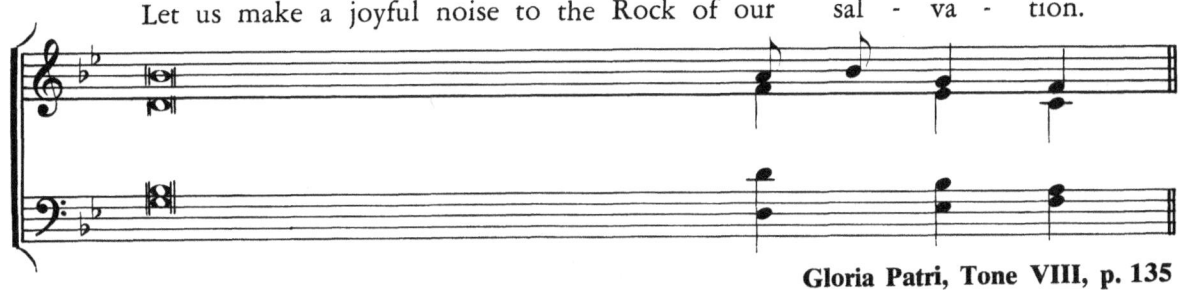

Gloria Patri, Tone VIII, p. 135

The Intervenient Chants

The Twenty-fifth Sunday After Trinity

The Introit

A. Have mercy upon me, O Lord, for I am in trouble: deliver me from the hand of mine enemies and from them that persecute me. Let me not be ashamed, O Lord: for I have called upon Thee.

PSALM   TONE II

In Thee, O Lord, do I put my trust: Let me never be ashamed.

Gloria Patri, Tone II, p. 132

The Intervenient Chants

THE GRADUAL

Thine enemies roar in the midst of Thy congregations:

The Twenty-sixth Sunday After Trinity

The Introit

Hear my prayer, O God: give ear to the words of my mouth.

PSALM   **TONE IV**

He shall re-ward evil to mine en-e-mies: cut them off in Thy truth.

Gloria Patri, Tone IV, p. 133

The Intervenient Chants

THE GRADUAL

He shall call to the heav-ens from a-bove and to the earth that He may judge His peo-ple. ℣ The heav-ens shall de-clare His righ-teous-ness:

THE ALLELUIA

for God is Judge Him-self. Al-le-lu-ia! Al-le-lu-ia!

℣ The ran-somed of the Lord shall come to Zi-on with ev-er-last-ing

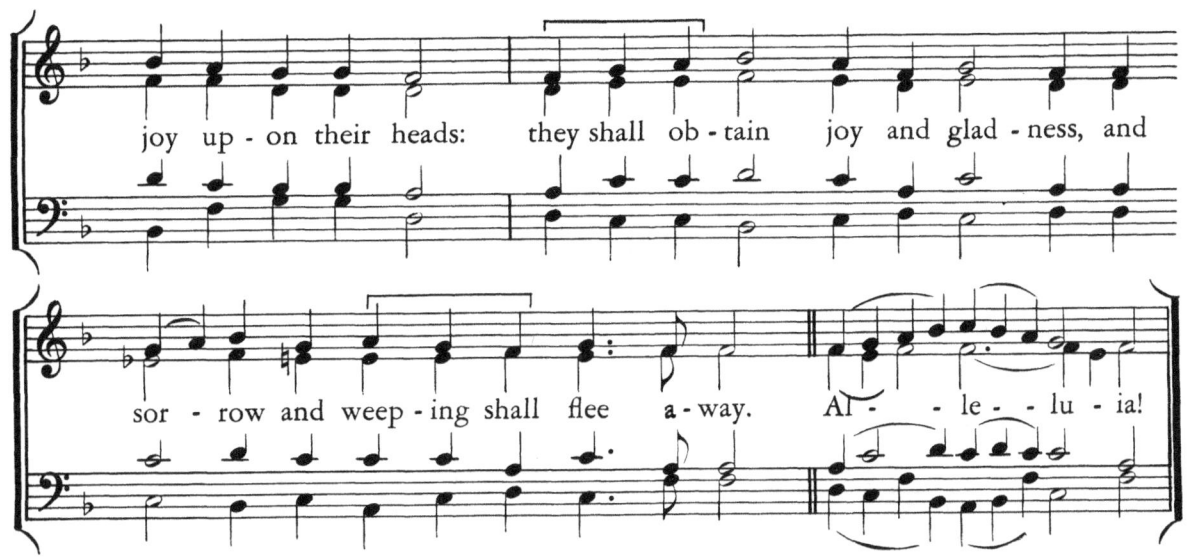

The Twenty-seventh Sunday After Trinity

The Introit

(The Introit for the Twenty-third Sunday After Trinity shall be used on the last Sunday after Trinity in each year, p. 120)

The Introit (alternate)

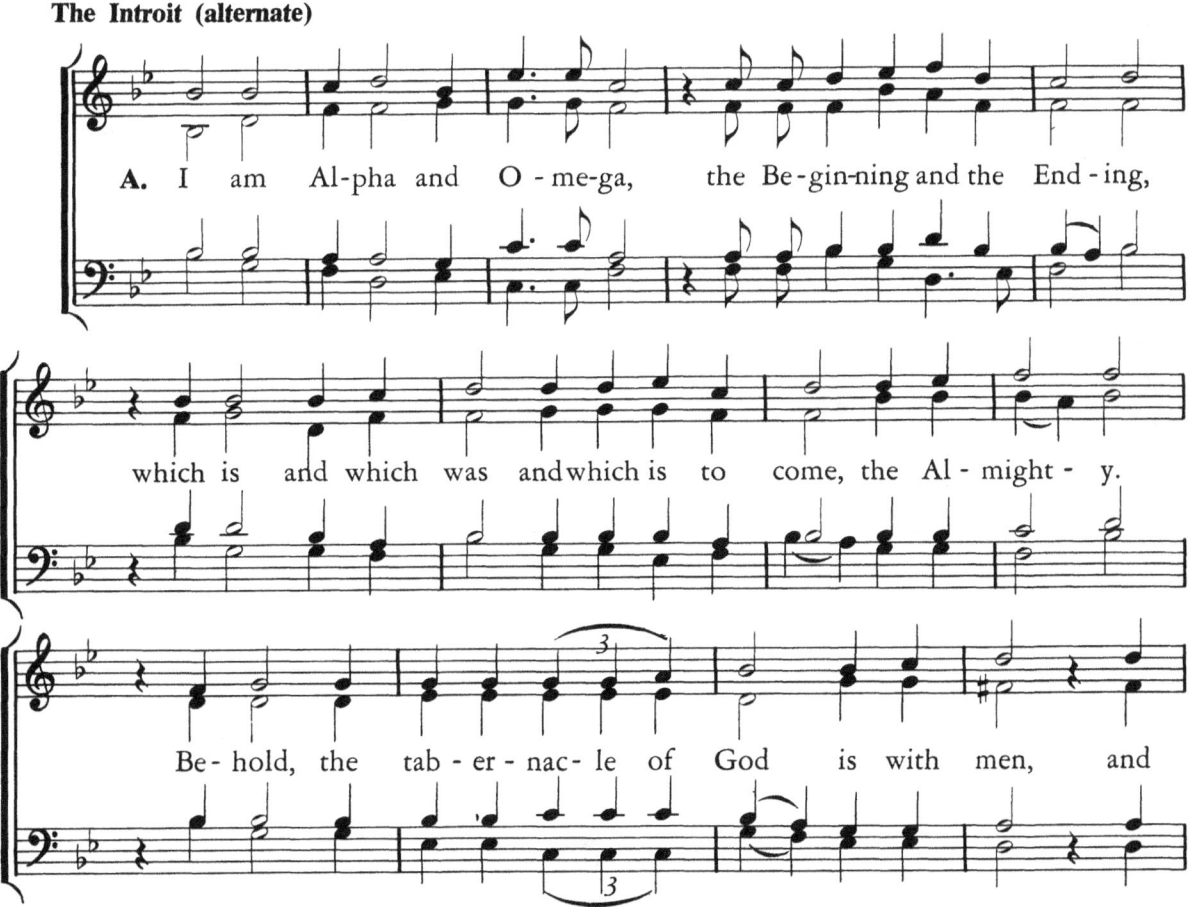

The Intervenient Chants

THE GRADUAL

In all places where I record My name I will come unto thee: and bless thee, saith your God. ℣ How amiable are Thy tabernacles: O Lord of hosts!

THE ALLELUIA

Alleluia! Alleluia! ℣ Yea, the sparrow hath found an house and the swallow a nest for herself, where she may lay her young: even Thine altars, O Lord of hosts, my King and my God. Alleluia!

Tone I

Repeat the Antiphon

Tone II

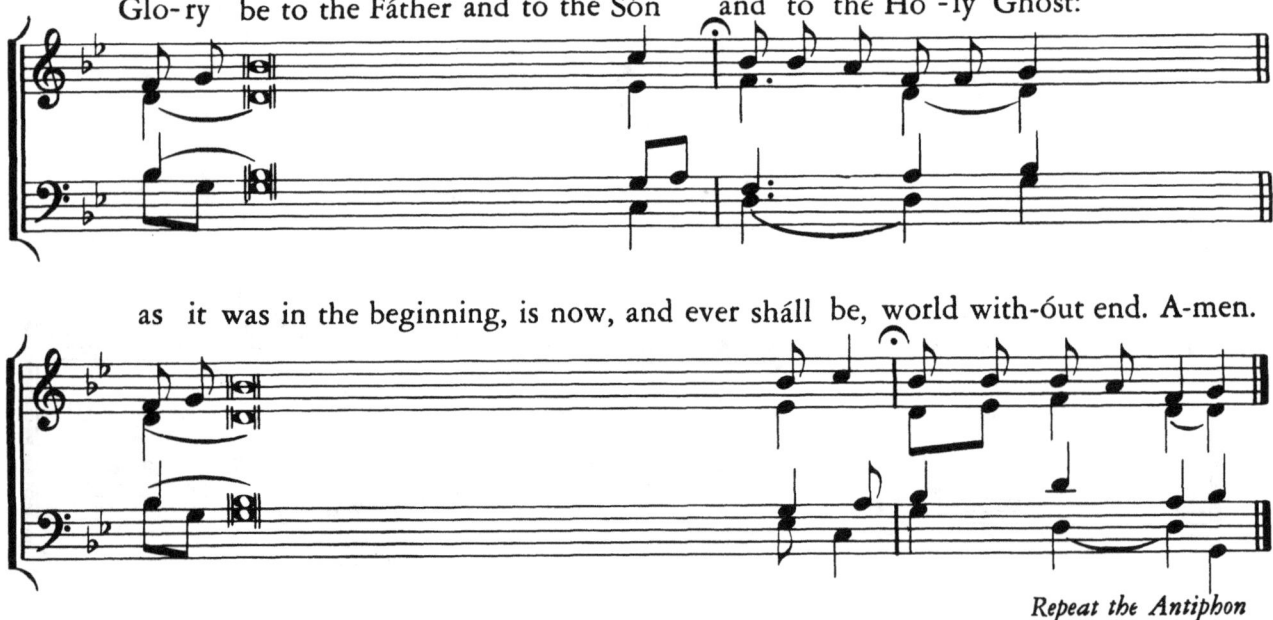

Repeat the Antiphon

Tone I

Repeat the Antiphon

Tone II

Repeat the Antiphon

Tone III

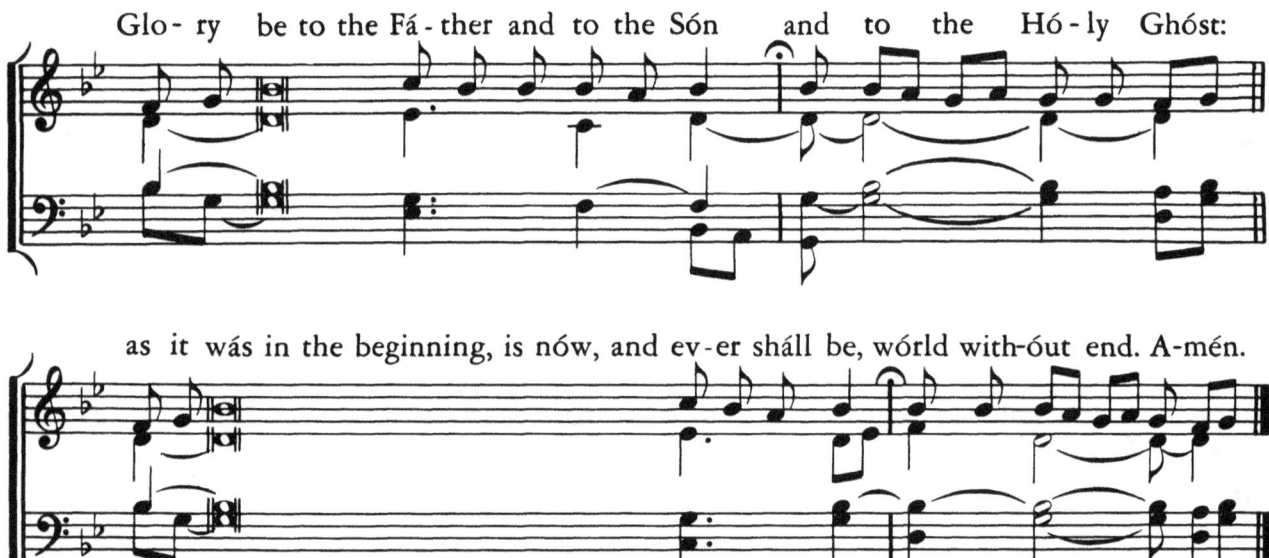

Repeat the Antiphon

Tone IV

Repeat the Antiphon

Tone V

Repeat the Antiphon

Tone VI

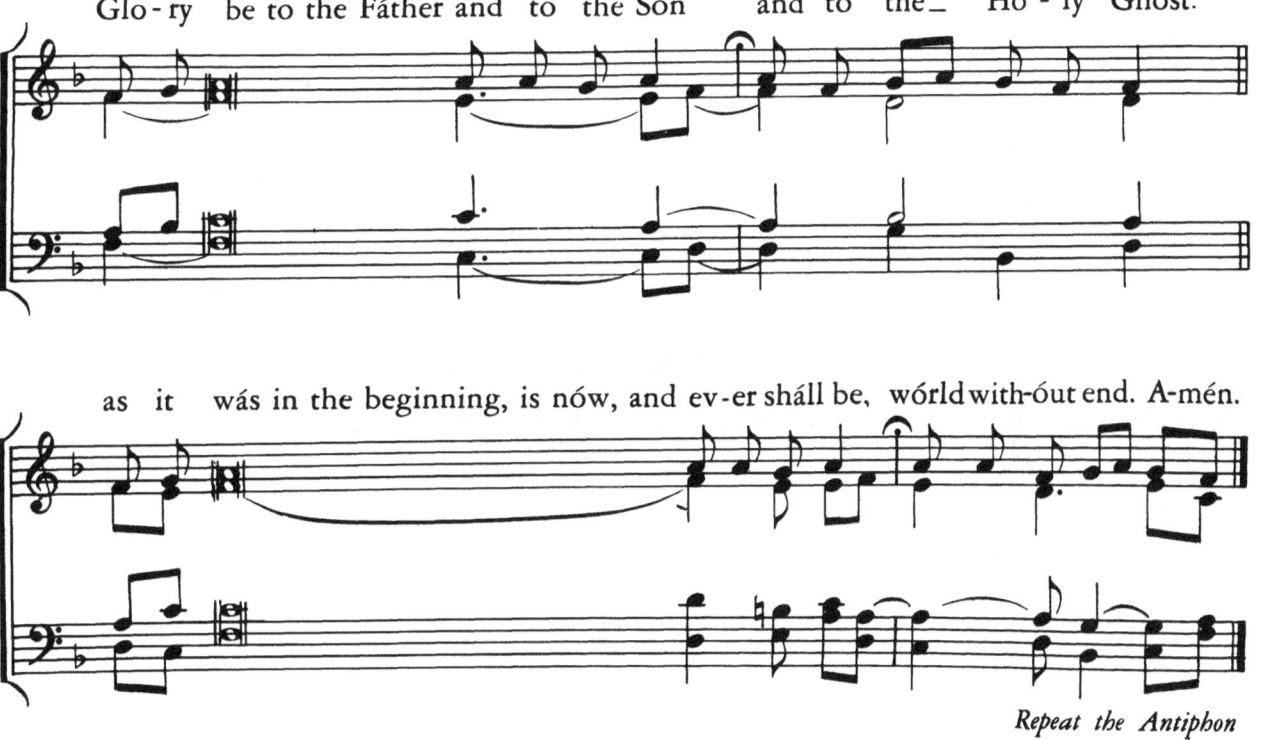

Repeat the Antiphon

Tone VII

Repeat the Antiphon

Tone VIII

Repeat the Antiphon

Tone III

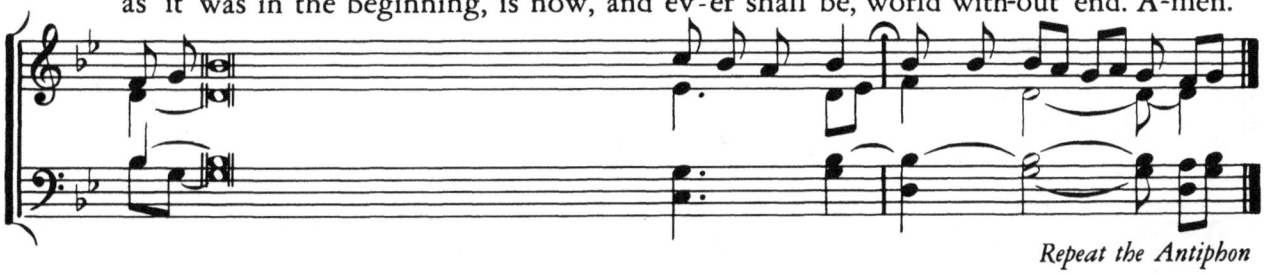

Repeat the Antiphon

Tone IV

Repeat the Antiphon

Tone V

Repeat the Antiphon

Tone VI

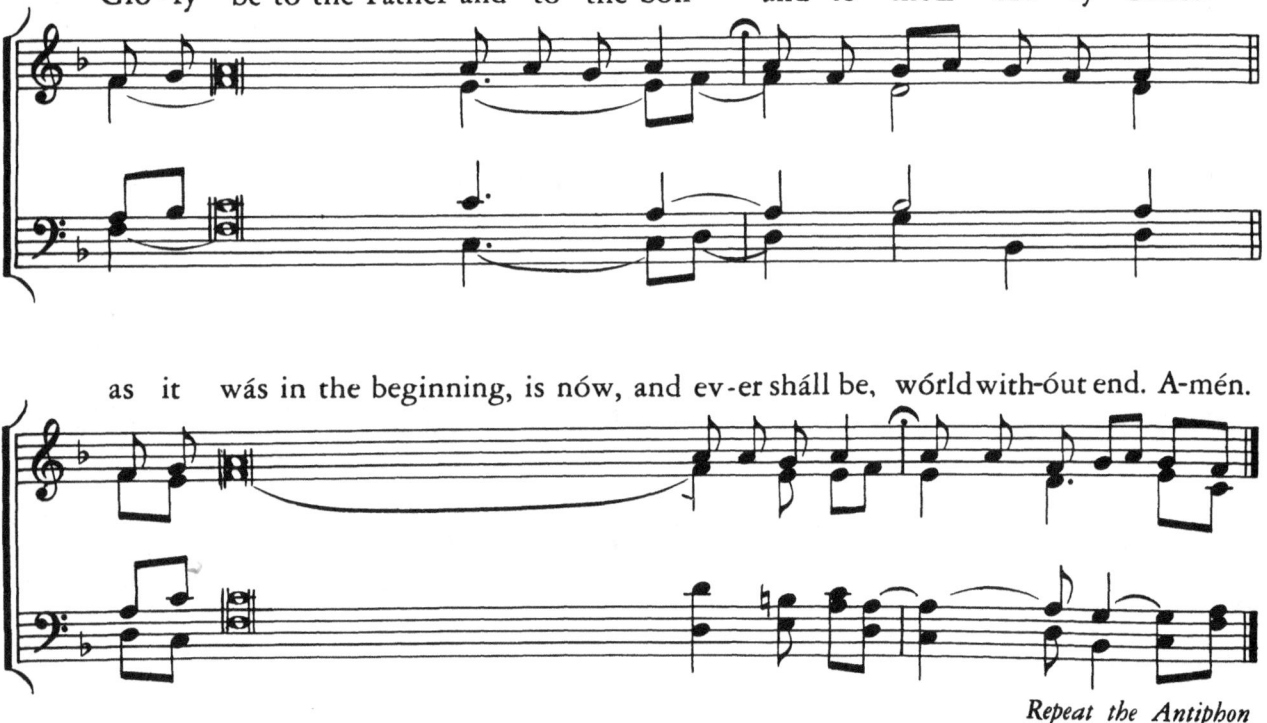

Repeat the Antiphon

Tone VII

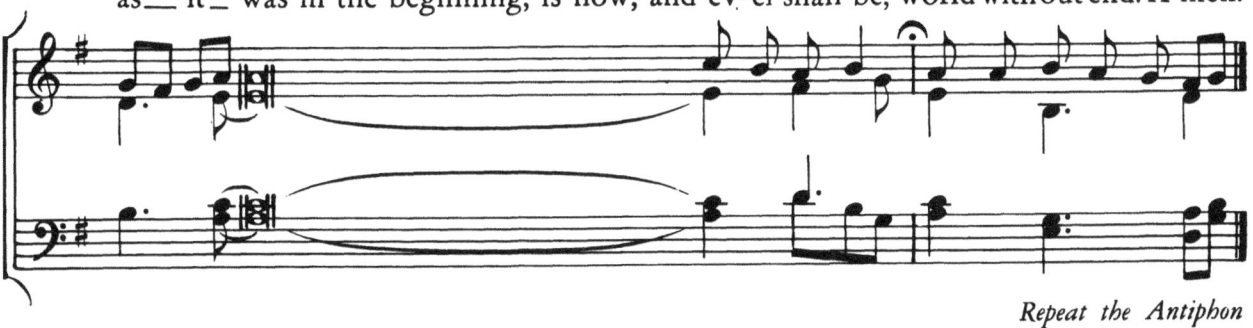

Repeat the Antiphon

Tone VIII

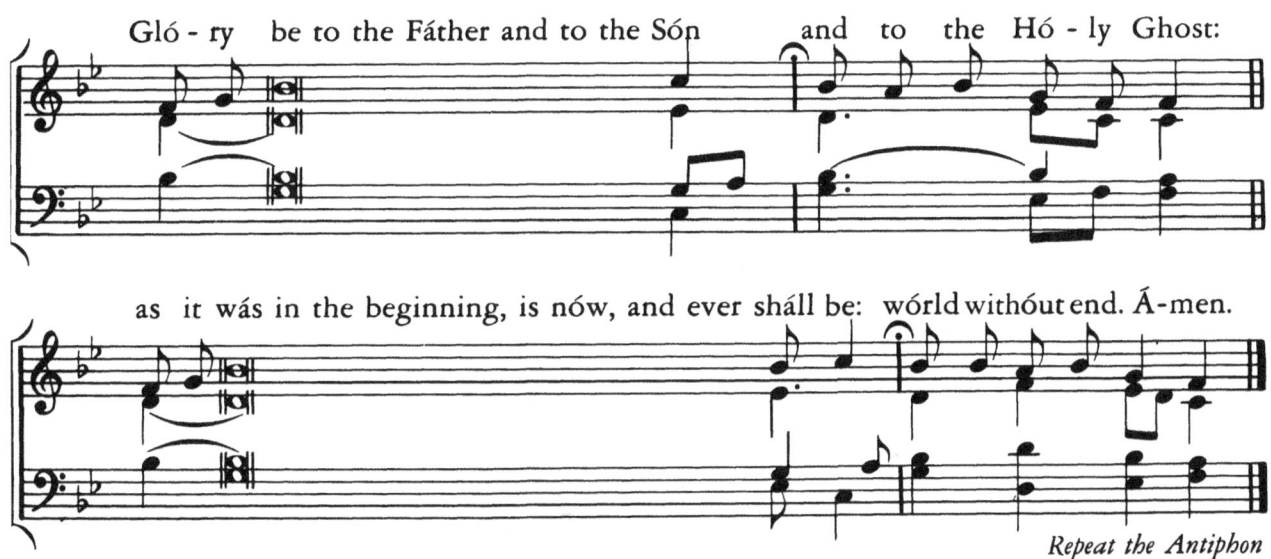

Repeat the Antiphon

www.ingramcontent.com/pod-product-compliance
Lightning Source LLC
Chambersburg PA
CBHW080923170426
43201CB00016B/2245